ABC OF VAT
AND
CUSTOMS AND EXCISE TERMS

ABC OF VAT
AND
CUSTOMS AND EXCISE TERMS

Gavin McFarlane LLM, PhD, Barrister

Member of the Taxation Unit at Titmuss Sainer & Webb
Member of the Institute of Export

BLACKSTONE
PRESS LIMITED

First published in Great Britain 1992 by Blackstone Press Limited,
9–15 Aldine Street, London W12 8AW. Telephone 081-740 1173

© G. McFarlane, 1992

ISBN: 1 85431 163 8

British Library Cataloguing in Publication Data
A CIP catalogue record for this book is available from the British
Library

Typeset by: Style Photosetting Ltd, Mayfield, East Sussex
Printed by: Redwood Press Ltd, Melksham, Wiltshire

Preface

The activities of the Department of Customs and Excise now impact on virtually the whole community. The application of value added tax continues to increase, and there can be few people who are not affected by it, either as taxable persons or consumers. Indeed the whole range of indirect taxes administered by the Department has assumed increasing importance as the fiscal burden is being gradually shifted on to them, and away from direct taxation.

Industries affected by excise and revenue duties, together with the import and export trades, have over the centuries developed highly specialised jargons in connection with their work with Customs and Excise. All concerned are having to familiarise themselves with the new terms deriving from the European Community, and this process will continue as we move towards harmonisation.

It is hoped that this book will prove a handy work of reference to all those who now have to deal with VAT and customs and excise matters. It should also be useful to members of the Department, who will need to be familiar with a terminology which is sometimes centuries old. Customs officers also need a basic knowledge of general commercial and legal terms, and accordingly some of the more commonly met expressions have been included.

Michelle Fraser has produced a typescript of great clarity in a remarkably short time, and working with Blackstone Press has as usual been a pleasure.

GMcF
November 1991

A

abandonment of claim. The reliquishment by one side to a civil action of its claim against the other party.

absolute bill of sale. A bill of sale (**q.v.**) not given as security for money which vests the property absolutely in the grantee (**q.v.**), although the grantor (**q.v.**) keeps possession.

absolute offence. A criminal offence of so-called strict liability, in which no element of intention is needed in order to prove guilt.

abroad. For customs purposes, in a country outside the United Kingdom.

abuse of process. Something done by the prosecution in a criminal trial which seriously prejudices the possibility of the accused successfully defending himself.

acceptable seal. A seal satisfying customs requirements which may be used to secure vehicles and parts of plant for revenue control purposes.

accepting house. The business of guaranteeing payment of debts by accepting bills drawn on them by the sellers of goods.

acceptor. The term applied after acceptance to the person (for example a bank) called on to make a payment under a cheque or bill of exchange.

accession. A period during which new member states gradually align their procedures with the rest of the European Community (**q.v.**).

accession compensatory amount (ACA). A charge applied at import or export to adjust price levels and prevent currency fluctuations in agricultural trade between a new member state of the European Community and the rest of the Community during a transitional period.

accident. A defence which may be successful in criminal cases where *mens rea* (**q.v.**) is required, but will not necessarily be effective in strict liability or absolute offences (**q.v.**).

accommodation bill. A negotiable instrument put into circulation without any consideration having been given, in order to assist or accommodate the person principally involved.

accord and satisfaction. An agreement between persons who originally made a contract that it shall be carried out in a different way, and that no legal action will result in consequence.

accompanied baggage. In relation to a person entering the United Kingdom, baggage which he brings with him when he enters.

accountant. The supply of services of an accountant is treated as supplied where received for the purposes of VAT.

Accountant-General. The official who holds funds paid to the credit of any matter in the Supreme Court of Judicature.

account payee only. A cheque with this crossing on it may only be paid into the account of the person specified. The bank receiving it is negligent if it pays it into any other account.

accounting centre. A Customs and Excise office where customs entries are processed into the Customs and Excise accounts system.

account sales. Goods, usually perishable, imported on consignment and valued for customs purposes by reference to the price achieved when sold in the European Community (**q.v.**).

accretion. The addition of new territory to the existing territory of a state by operation of nature, such as the emergence of a volcanic island like Surtsey off the coast of Iceland.

Acme T Lock Seal. An official Customs seal for the securing of goods. It consists of a metal strip inserted into a flat locking box.

acquittal. A verdict in a criminal case that the facts alleged against the person accused are not proved, and that accordingly he should not be convicted.

act of bankruptcy. One of a number of acts committed by a debtor in respect of which a bankruptcy petition may be founded. An example would be a fraudulent transfer of part of his property.

act of God. An act of fate or the workings of nature which has caused some loss, damage or injury.

Act of Parliament. A written law which has passed through first, second and third readings in both Houses of Parliament, and has received the Royal Assent (**q.v.** statute).

act of state. (1) An exercise of power by the sovereign which cannot be questioned in a court of law. (2) A defence to an action in an English court in respect of an act committed abroad by a Crown servant.

action *in personam*. A case against a person, as opposed to a case for the recovery of a thing or goods.

actionable per se. Applied to an action which can be brought without proof of damage.

active partner. A member of a partnership (**q.v.**) who assumes executive responsibility for the business.

actual charge. A charge to excise duty based on the litres of alcohol in the spirits actually produced.

actual loss. The situation where no part of the subject-matter of a policy of insurance remains in existence.

***actus reus*.** An act which is forbidden for the purposes of criminal law.

additional duty on flour. A variable rate which only comes into force where a maximum amount for duty and variable charge (**q.v.**) purposes is shown in the Tariff (**q.v.**). An additional duty for sugar also exists.

address for service. An address nominated by a party to a case, at which any document for him may be left.

***ad hoc*.** For a specific case, in the sense of an arrangement or action taken to deal with a particular situation.

***ad idem*.** In complete agreement.

***ad infinitum*.** For ever.

***ad litem*.** For the purposes of the case, as in guardian ad litem (**q.v.**).

***ad valorem* duty.** A duty payable on goods calculated as a percentage of their value.

***ad valorem* freight.** A charge for shipping on goods by reference to a stated percentage of their value.

adjacent zone. In international law, water outside the territorial limits of a particular state, where special interests may be claimed.

3

adjourned *sine die*. Adjourned without a date being fixed for the next hearing of a case; therefore adjourned indefinitely.

administration order. A court order for the administration of the estate of a person who cannot pay the terms of a court judgment made against him.

administrative law. The rules covering areas of legal control exercised by agencies other than courts which have the right to administer law. Much of this is concerned with tribunals.

administrative tribunals. Bodies outside the ordinary judicial system of courts, set up under Acts of Parliament with judicial or similar powers.

administrator. In certain circumstances an administrator may be separately registered for VAT.

Admiralty Court. Until 1873, the court which dealt with Admiralty matters. They were then transferred to the Probate, Divorce and Admiralty Division of the High Court.

Admiralty Court of the Cinque Ports. A special court sitting to hear maritime matters arising within the jurisdiction of the Cinque Ports.

admiralty law. The body of law arising out of shipping and maritime matters, including salvage and collisions at sea.

admission. The acknowledgment by one side of a case to the other side of the truth of certain matters alleged.

advance documentation scheme. A scheme under which regular importers can lodge the documentation for customs clearance in advance of the arrival of an air parcel, thus reducing delivery time.

advance fixing certificate. A certificate granted on request by the Intervention Board for Agricultural Produce (**q.v.**). Its purpose is to fix rates of refund, levy or Monetary Compensatory Amount (**q.v.**) for imports or exports in the future.

advance freight. A sum to be paid in advance, in respect of the carriage of goods by sea.

advance payment. A system under which the export refund (**q.v.**) can be paid in advance of proof that goods have left the European Community or reached their destination.

advertising services. The supply of advertising services is treated as supplied where received for VAT purposes.

advocate. One who presents a case orally, as a barrister or solicitor; in Scotland, a member of the Faculty of Advocates, equivalent to a barrister in England or Wales. VAT supplies by an advocate in Scotland are treated as taking place on the basis of cash received.

aerodrome. Any area of land or water designed, equipped, set apart or commonly used for affording facilities for the landing and departure of aircraft.

affidavit. A document sworn on oath before a commissioner to administer oaths.

affiliate. A commercial organisation which is subject to the control or influence of another commercial organisation.

affirmation. The alternative to the swearing of an oath (**q.v.**) in judicial proceedings, either where the person making the declaration does not wish to swear on the basis of religious belief, or where it is not practicable to administer the appropriate oath.

affreightment. The carriage of goods by sea in return for reward.

agency. The engagement by one person of an intermediary to bring about contractual relations with a third person.

agency by implication. An agency inferred in certain cases from the conduct of the persons concerned.

agency by ratification. The situation where a person subsequently adopts acts done on his behalf by another person which were not properly authorised.

agency of necessity. Where in an emergency the powers of an agent are by implication of law conferred on a particular person.

agent. An intermediary engaged by one person to bring about contractual relations with another. In certain circumstances he may be substituted for his principal as the person accountable for VAT.

agent's advice note. Document giving full particulars of cargo sent by an exporter to his forwarding agent.

agreed value clause. A provision in a bill of lading limiting the carrier's liability to a fixed sum.

agricultural activity. For VAT relief for imported goods: includes stock-farming, bee-keeping, horticulture and forestry.

agricultural levy. A charge made under the Common Agricultural Policy (**q.v.**) on goods imported from non-European countries, to compensate for the difference between European Community and world prices.

agricultural tenancy. A letting of premises under the terms of their employment to someone engaged in agricultural work.

aiding and abetting. Assisting in a crime, now usually as a principal in the second degree.

aids for the handicapped. Certain aids for the handicapped are zero-rated for VAT (Sch. 5, VATA).

air conditioning. Zero-rated for VAT as fuel and power (Sch. 5, VATA).

aircraft. For customs purposes, includes all balloons, kites, gliders, airships and flying machines. If over 8,000 kilograms, and not designed or adapted for recreation or pleasure, it is zero-rated for VAT (Sch. 5, VATA).

aircraft mortgage. For VAT purposes, a mortgage registered in accordance with legislation by virtue of which an aircraft is made security for a loan.

aircraft operator. The person having the management or overall control of an aircraft (**q.v.**) at a particular time.

aircraft stores. Goods for use in an aircraft or for retail sale to people carried in them.

air crew. Persons assigned by an operator to duty on an aircraft during flight time.

airgun. Second-hand airguns are not eligible for VAT treatment under the margin scheme (**q.v.**) for firearms unless registered as firearms.

airside. The area of an airport subject to customs control when an outgoing passenger has passed through customs.

air waybill. A contractual document between shipper and carrier regulating the carriage of goods by air.

alcohol. For purposes of customs and excise, ethyl alcohol.

alcoholic liquor. For purposes of customs and excise, spirits, methylated spirits, and any fermented liquor other than wash (**q.v.**).

alcoholic liquor duty. An excise duty on alcoholic liquor (**q.v.**).

ale. Originally applied to beer brewed without hops; but now included in the legal definition of beer.

alibi. The contention by a person accused of a criminal offence that he was elsewhere at the relevant time.

alibi warning. Notice which the defence is obliged to give to the prosecution of its intention to plead an alibi.

alien enemy. A foreigner with whose country war has broken out. He enjoys no rights or privileges in the United Kingdom in consequence.

alien friend. A foreigner who enjoys most rights of a citizen of the United Kingdom, except that he cannot vote or hold official office.

all round guaging. The calculation of the contents of a cask from its measured dimensions.

allonge. A slip of paper attached to a bill of exchange (**q.v.**) on which a series of indorsers add their signatures.

alongside date. The date when a ship is ready to take on cargo for exportation.

ambassador. A person exempt from civil and criminal proceedings together with certain categories of staff of foreign embassies and equivalent persons, by virtue of Britain's recognition of international convention.

amendment. An alteration to a legal document or draft, or to a bill on its way through Parliament.

American Foreign Trade Definitions (AFTD). An American system of standardised contractual terms for international trade, sometimes used instead of INCOTERMS (**q.v.**).

American roulette. A game in respect of which gaming licence duty is payable for any premises on which it is played.

angostura bitters. An aromatic flavouring essence, generally deemed not to be spirits for purposes of customs and excise.

animal feeding stuffs. Supplies of animal feeding stuffs are zero-rated for VAT (Sch. 5, VATA).

annual accounting. A scheme under which a taxable person may account for and pay VAT on an annual rather than a quarterly or monthly basis.

annual general meeting. A meeting which every company must hold each year, and which must take place within 15 months of the previous annual general meeting.

annual return. A document which a company must file each year setting out particulars of addresses, directors, members, indebtedness and capital.

antecedents. Details given to a court about to sentence a person guilty of a criminal offence about his record or background.

ante-dated cheque. A cheque bearing a date earlier than the date on which it was made out.

anti-dumping duty. A charge levied by an importing country to counteract goods entering which appear to have been unfairly subsidised in the country of production.

antiques. Supplies of antiques are subject to a margin scheme (**q.v.**) and only liable to VAT on the difference between acquisition and disposal prices.

anti-trust legislation. A branch of United States law designed to ensure fair competition; it affects contracts between American and non-American companies which infringe its principles.

Anton Pillar Order. A court order allowing the applicant to search premises for evidence, and seize it. Used to combat material infringing copyright.

appellant. A person who brings an appeal, particularly to a VAT tribunal (**q.v.**).

appraisement. The valuation of a ship or its cargo for the purposes of salvage.

appraiser. Someone who carries out the calling or occupation of appraisement (**q.v.**) or valuation.

appropriation. The earmarking of money under parliamentary authorisation for funding public expenditure.

appropriation accounts. Accounts made by the various departments of state of the manner in which grants voted to them by Parliament have been spent.

appropriation in aid. The setting off by a department of state or ministry of money it has received from outside sources against money it would normally be due to receive from the Exchequer.

approved furnace operator. A person approved for the purposes of hydrocarbon oil duty (**q.v.**) to burn light oil (**q.v.**) as furnace fuel.

approved hours. The days and hours of opening approved for each individual bonded warehouse (**q.v.**).

approved inland clearance depot. Any inland premises approved by the Commissioners for the clearance of goods for customs and excise purposes.

approved route. A route which Customs and Excise may designate for the movement of goods across the Irish land boundary.

approved wharf. A place approved by Customs and Excise for the loading and unloading of goods.

aqua vitae. Originally applied for duty purposes to plain spirits distilled in the Scottish Lowlands, as opposed to 'usque baugh' distilled in the Highlands.

arbitrage. The technique of dealing by taking profits from known price differences existing in different places at the same time.

arbitration. A system of settling disputes outside the formal scheme of the civil courts. It is frequently used in commercial matters.

arbitrator. A kind of umpire or referee who with the agreement of both parties can settle a dispute outside the court system.

armed forces. For customs purposes, the Royal Navy, the Royal Marines, the Regular Army, the Royal Air Force, and any reserve or auxiliary force of any of those services which has been called out on permanent or actual service, or embodied.

arrack. For duty purposes, a spirit distilled from toddy, rice or palm pulp.

arraignment. Procedure in the Crown Court by which the statement of the offence in an indictment is read to the person accused, and he is asked how he pleads.

arrest. The apprehension of a person so that he may answer a criminal charge.

arrestable offence. A crime in respect of which an unauthorised person may make an arrest without warrant.

arrest with a warrant. Arrest by a police officer or other authorised person under a warrant issued by a justice of the peace after hearing evidence on oath that a crime has been committed.

arrest without a warrant. Apprehension by a police officer or other authorised person for a criminal offence defined as an arrestable offence and therefore one for which arrest without warrant can be made.

arrival. In relation to vessels, means the anchoring, berthing or mooring within the limits of a port.

articles of association. A company document defining the rights of its members as between themselves, and against the company, and the delegation of powers to the directors.

articles of partnership. A document embodying the conditions governing a particular partnership relationship.

artificial person. A legal person other than a human being, for example, a corporation.

assault. The attempt to apply unlawful force to the body of another person, and causing that person to fear violence.

assaulting a customs officer. A statutory offence which may be tried on indictment in the Crown Court.

assay office. An office set up for the hall-marking of gold and silver plate in London and certain provincial cities.

assessed taxes. Formerly applied to duties assessed according to the number of taxable articles kept by a particular person. An example was the notorious window tax.

assessment. A document recording the raising by Customs and Excise of an amount of VAT which they allege to be due from a person.

assessor. A person with special skills who may be appointed to assist a judge in certain types of case.

assigned matter. Anything in relation to which Customs and Excise are required under any enactment to perform any duty.

assignment. A transfer of rights which has legal effect.

assimilated products. Certain partly processed materials classed as basic products (**q.v.**), as they are freely interchangeable in manufacture with certain basic products.

association registration. The separate registration for VAT of an association, as opposed to the members of that association.

assurance. The undertaking by one person (the assurer) to pay money or confer a benefit on another person (the assured) on the happening of an event certain to take place in the future, generally the death of a specified person.

assured. A person standing to benefit under a contract of assurance (**q.v.**).

assurer. A person undertaking to pay a certain sum or confer another benefit on another person (the assured) on the taking place of an event certain to happen in the future, generally the death of a nominated person.

ATA carnet. A carnet for temporary admission facilitating customs clearance of certain temporary importations and exportations.

attachment of earnings. The power to enforce a financial penalty or court order by direct deduction from wages or salary.

attempt. A step taken towards the commission of a substantive criminal offence, which in certain circumstances may itself amount to a crime.

attendance. The times at which a customs officer or customs establishment is on duty.

attendance centre. A person under 21 may be sentenced to attend such a centre to forfeit his/her leisure, and to be guided to useful recreational activities.

attenuation charge. A charge to excise duty based on the litres of alcohol capable of being produced from the attenuation of the wort or wash.

attest. To sign as a witness to the signature of another person.

attestation. The act of witnessing a signature on a document. In the case of a will the document would be invalid without it.

Attorney-General. One of the two Law Officers of the Crown, and a political appointment. He is the Head of the Bar of England and Wales, who advises certain government departments, and undertakes certain prosecutions for the Crown.

Attorney-General's reference. The procedure by which a point of law arising in a criminal case where the accused has been acquitted may be taken to the Court of Appeal by the Attorney-General for its opinion.

attribution. A method of relating credit for input tax (**q.v.**) to taxable supplies (**q.v.**).

auction. A public sale of goods or estate by stroke of hammer or other recognised manner at which the highest bidder is deemed to be the purchaser.

auctioneer. A person offering goods or property for sale by competitive bidding at which the purchaser is deemed to be the highest bidder.

audience. The right to address a court in legal proceedings, generally confined to the party him/herself, or a barrister or solicitor acting on his/her behalf.

audit. The periodic examination of account books by an auditor (**q.v.**), to verify that they are correctly made up.

auditors. Qualified accountants independent of a company who must be retained to report on its accounts.

auditors' report. A statement which must be given to the general meeting of company each year giving the opinion of the auditors (**q.v.**) as to whether the accounts have been properly kept.

aulnager. The holder of a medieval office for the measurement and taxation of imported cloth.

authenticated receipt procedure. A receipt given by a person supplying standard rated construction services. It may be treated as a tax invoice for the purpose of credit for input tax.

authorised capital. The nominal value of shares which a limited company is permitted by its memorandum of association (**q.v.**) to issue (also known as nominal capital).

authorised methylator. Any distiller, rectifier or compounder (**q.v.**) authorised to methylate or mix spirits.

authorised person. For VAT purposes, an authorised person is any person acting under the authority of the Commissioners of Customs and Excise.

automatism. A condition whereby a person has no mental control over his/her movements.

autonomic legislation. The power of an autonomous body such as a club or a professional association to make rules governing its members.

autrefois acquit. A contention by a person accused of a criminal offence that he/she had already been found not guilty of a charge.

autrefois convict. A contention by a person accused of a criminal offence that he/she had already been tried for it and convicted.

average. In contracts of marine insurance, an expression meaning loss or damage.

average clause. A clause in an insurance policy providing that if the value of property exceeds the amount for which it is insured, the insurer is only liable in the proportion which the sum insured bears to the property.

aviation gasoline. Light oil specially produced and delivered as fuel for aircraft and not normally used in road vehicles.

awards. Certain awards of a symbolic nature may be entitled to personal relief (**q.v.**) from duty and/or VAT on importation.

B

baccarat. A game in respect of which gaming licence duty is payable on any premises on which it is played.

bachelor duty. A tax imposed in 1695 on every bachelor over the age of 25, at a rate on a sliding scale according to his social position. It was abolished in 1706.

back freight. An amount due to a shipowner in a contract for the carriage of goods by sea where goods have been carried beyond their original destination because it was not possible to deliver them.

bad debt relief. A scheme for the refunding of VAT to taxable persons who have paid output tax (**q.v.**) on suppliers, in certain circumstances where they have incurred a bad debt.

bail. The grant of liberty to an accused person pending trial, generally subject to conditions.

bail by the police. The release of a person arrested without warrant on a less serious charge by the officer in charge of a police station where that person will not be brought before a court within 24 hours.

bailee. The person to whom goods are delivered on condition that they will be returned to the person who delivered them when the purpose of the delivery (bailment) has been fulfilled.

bailiff. A court official responsible for serving court documents, and enforcing its judgments by taking away goods under execution.

bailment. A delivery of goods by one person, the bailor, to another person, the bailee, on condition that they shall be returned as soon as the purpose of the bailment is fulfilled.

14

bailor. A person who delivers goods to another person (bailee) on condition that they will be returned when the purpose of the delivery (bailment) has been fulfilled.

balance of advantages. A principle under which advantages obtained from the trading of concessions in trade negotiations should broadly be balanced between the participants.

balance of payments. The balance of credit and debit transactions on a country's external account, including both goods and services.

balance of trade. A country's balance of import and export of goods.

balance sheet. A statement which the directors of a company must put before its members each year in general meeting, giving a true picture of its affairs.

Baltic exchange. A London market for dealing in grain to be delivered at some time in the future.

bank notes. Issues of notes by banks to bearer on demand are zero-rated for VAT (Sch. 5, VATA).

banker's books. A bank's official record of its customers' accounts, production of which in evidence may in some circumstances be enforced by court order.

banker's confirmed credit. An arrangement between the purchaser of goods and his banker that a sum of money will be paid to the seller of the goods on presentment to the bank of certain documents of authority.

banker's draft. A draft for a sum of money drawn on a particular office of a bank which is payable immediately to the person due to receive it.

banking services. The supply of banking services is treated as supplied where received for VAT purposes.

bar box. A secure box for containing surplus aircraft stores (**q.v.**), which is capable of being secured by a seal.

Baron of Exchequer. A judge of the old Exchequer court, dealing with revenue cases.

barratry. A deliberate act of fraud or wrong-doing by a ship's master and/or crew, by which the owners or charterers of a ship are damaged.

barrister. VAT supplies by a barrister are treated as taking place on the basis of cash received.

barter. A contract to pay for the purchase of goods with other goods rather than money.

basic products. For purposes of the European Community (**q.v.**), basic products of the soil, of stock farming and fisheries, together with goods resulting from first stage processing of certain basic products.

bastard sugar. For duty purposes, lump sugar broken into pieces.

bastard wine. For duty purposes, wine which has been mixed or sweetened.

bearer. The person in possession of a particular document. Some documents such as bearer bills and bearer debentures confer a benefit which may be claimed by any person in possession.

bearer cheque. A cheque which can be negotiated merely by delivery.

bearer security (bearer bond). Stocks or shares the title to which is evidenced by a bond conferring ownership on the person holding it for the time.

beef clawback. A recovery of slaughter premium applicable to certain exports of live bovine animals and beef.

beer. A term which includes ale, porter, stout and any other liquor sold or described as beer and having a strength over 1.2%.

beetroot distillery. Premises in which the distillation of spirits from beetroots was commenced experimentally in 1856 at Farningham and eleven other centres. It was abandoned in 1863 as unremunerative.

Belfast airport. An area which has been designated a free zone (**q.v.**) for the purpose of duty and tax.

belligerent. A state actively engaged in war with another state.

belongings. Goods other than motor vehicles kept for personal use, and subject to certain reliefs.

Benelux. The three countries of Belgium, Holland and Luxembourg considered or acting together.

best evidence. A rule of the law of evidence that best means of proof which the nature of the case allows must be given.

bet. A payment made for the chance of winning any money or money's worth, where the payer has the power of selection (whether exercised or not), which may determine the winner. Bets are exempt from VAT (Sch. 6, VATA).

betting duty. A tax charged on bets made with a bookmaker, now only in betting-shops. On-course betting is no longer subject to the tax.

betting duty account. An account which must be kept by a bookmaker in a special book issued by Customs and Excise.

betting office licence. A document issued by a local licensing authority to the holder of a bookmaker's permit (**q.v.**).

big six. A game in respect of which gaming licence duty is payable for any premises on which it is played.

bilateralism. Trade negotiations between two countries leading to the establishment of privileges between them which are not extended to others.

bill of exchange. An unconditional written order addressed by one person to another, and signed by the person giving it, which requires the person to whom it is addressed to pay either on demand or at a particular time in the future a certain sum of money to either a particular person or his order, or to the person holding the bill of exchange.

bill of exchange policy. A form of bad debt insurance covering losses on bills of exchange drawn by the insured person.

bill of health. A certificate of freedom from disease issued on request at the port of clearance to the master of a ship sailing to a foreign destination in which quarantine regulations are observed.

bill of lading. A document recording the loading of goods onto a ship, with particulars of the terms agreed as to their carriage.

bill of lading in blank. A bill of lading (**q.v.**) which may be freely transferred from hand to hand.

bill of sale. Effected in connection with a loan, so as to transfer ownership of the object put up as security to the lender, while possession of the object stays with the borrower.

bill of sight. A provisional customs entry allowing an importer to land and examine goods under surveillance when he has not sufficient information to make a declaration without examination.

bill of store. A Customs entry for the re-importation of goods which have been exported within the previous five years.

binding over. A power vested in magistrates to require a person to keep the peace and be of good behaviour. It does not depend on a conviction, and may be imposed on someone found not guilty.

Binding Tariff Information (**BTI**). A European Community system providing a common approach to the provision of tariff information by customs authorities.

bingo duty. An excise duty imposed on bingo played on premises licensed by the local gaming licensing committee, and elsewhere unless exempt.

bingo promoter. The person taking money in payment for cards or to whom the players look for payment of prizes.

Birmingham airport. An area which has been designated as a free zone (**q.v.**) for the purpose of duty and VAT.

birth duty. A tax imposed in 1695 on parents on a sliding scale according to their social standing in respect of the birth of every child. It was abolished in 1706.

black beer. Mum, spruce beer or Berlin white beer, or any other preparation of a similar character, whether or not fermented.

blackjack. A game in respect of which gaming licence duty is payable for any premises on which it is played.

blocked currency. The system adopted by certain states of paying money due to a foreign creditor into a special 'blocked' account, which the creditor can only use for a restricted range of purposes.

boarding station. A place appointed at every port in the United Kingdom at which ships arriving from or going abroad must be brought to for the boarding or landing of customs officers.

bona vacantia. Property without an owner, and which no one is entitled to inherit.

bond. A financial guarantee given to Customs and Excise to secure the payment of duty.

bonded distributor. For the purposes of hydrocarbon oil, a person who has given bond and been approved for the supply of oil in the course of trade.

bonded goods. Goods which for purposes of release from duty have been subject to the payment of a bond by way of security.

bonded user. A person who has given security by bond and received approval for certain uses of hydrocarbon oil (**q.v.**) or its supply.

bonds. The issue, transfer, receipt of or dealing with bonds is exempt from VAT (Sch. 6, VATA).

bonus shares. An issue of fully-paid up shares to a company's shareholders, issued from profits which have been retained in the past.

book debts. Those sums shown in a trader's accounts as being money due to him.

book entry. An entry made in accounts merely for the purposes of adjustment.

book value. The valuation of a property belonging to a business enterprise as it is given in its accounts.

booklets. Booklets are zero-rated for VAT (Sch. 5, VATA).

bookmaker's permit. A document issued by a local licensing authority, allowing the holder to act as a bookmaker.

books. Books are zero-rated for VAT (Sch. 5, VATA).

books duty. A customs duty on imported books first imposed in 1660, and abolished in 1861.

books of account. Records of receipts, expenditure, sales, purchases, assets and liabilities which a company is obliged to maintain in a proper manner.

boots. Protective boots for industrial use are zero-rated for VAT (Sch. 5, VATA).

bottomry bond. A form of security pledging a ship and/or its cargo for the repayment of money borrowed for the purposes of a voyage.

boule. A game for which gaming licence duty is payable for any premises on which it is played.

bound tariff. A tariff fixed in GATT (**q.v.**), schedules which can be altered only if compensation is negotiated.

box. In relation to the Continental Shelf, (**q.v.**) an area comprised by the North Sea, the Skagerrak, the Kattegat, the English Channel, and the area bounded by latitudes 48° 30'N and 61°N, and longitude 12°W.

breach of regulatory provision. A civil penalty in VAT law for the breach of one of a wide range of requirements in VAT regulations.

breach of walking possession agreement. A civil penalty in VAT law for allowing goods subject to a walking possession agreement to be removed from specified premises.

breaking bulk. The act of starting the unloading of a ship.

brewer. A person holding an excise licence to brew beer.

brewer for sale. A person holding an excise licence to brew beer for sale.

British Broadcasting Corporation. A body which may be entitled to a refund of VAT in certain circumstances under s.20, VATA.

British compounded spirits. Spirits which have in the United Kingdom been flavoured, or mixed with an ingredient or material, other than methylated spirits.

British ship. A ship wholly owned by a British subject or body corporate established under United Kingdom law, which has to be registered under the Merchant Shipping legislation.

British Standards Institution (BSI). The organisation authorised to draw up national standards in the United Kingdom.

brochures. Brochures are zero-rated for VAT (Sch. 5, VATA).

Brussels tariff nomenclature. The standard classification of goods for the purpose of customs tariffs which is most widely used internationally.

bub. A mixture of yeast and wort for promoting fermentation.

budget. A collection of proposals put forward by the Chancellor of the Exchequer to control the expenditure of the state, generally on an annual basis.

bulk clearance. Authorisation given to certain airline operators, to submit provisional schedules of expected departures, followed by final schedules of actual departures.

bullion. Unrefined gold and silver in dust, amalgam or lumps and bars, and refined gold or silver in bars.

burden of proof. The onus of establishing that a particular argument is correct.

burial. The disposal of the dead and the making of connected arrangements is exempt from VAT (Sch. 6, VATA).

burial duty. A tax imposed in 1695 on the burial of every person at a varying rate according to their social position. It was abolished in 1706.

business. Business for the purposes of VAT includes any trade or profession, also the provision of facilities by a club, association or organisation.

business entertainment. For VAT purposes, means entertainment, including any hospitality provided in connection with a business, except provision for employees (unless incidental to provision for others).

business name. The name or style under which any business is carried on, either as a company or partnership, or under a sole proprietor.

butlerage (also prisage). Wine taken by the King's Butler for the King's use from every ship bringing wine into the country.

C

C.A. attendance. Attendance (**q.v.**) by a Customs and Excise officer at places and times for which a charge is always made.

CAD (cash against documents). A procedure by which a bank will only hand over documents giving title to goods under a contract on receipt of money.

CAN (Customs assigned number). A system of allocating numbers for endorsement on export documentation so that statistical information can be collected.

C & F (cost and freight). A contract by which the seller undertakes to deliver goods on board a ship for a particular destination, and pay freight and unloading charges on arrival.

called-up capital. That section of the shareholding which has been called up on the shares issued. They are not therefore fully paid up, and liable to further calls.

calling aircraft. An aircraft flying between two foreign destinations which lands in the United Kingdom only in an emergency or for supplies, without loading or unloading freight or passengers.

calling ship. A ship coming from abroad into a foreign port only for bunkering or taking on stores, and which does not remain more than 24 hours.

candied peel. Zero-rated for VAT, as food of a kind used for human consumption (Sch. 5, VATA).

CAP charges. Charges arising from the Common Agricultural Policy (**q.v.**), such as levies, variable charges, monetary compensatory amounts, and accession compensatory amounts (all q.v.).

capital assets. The property owned by a limited company.

capital clause. The clause in a company's memorandum of association which sets out the amount of nominal capital with which a company is to be registered, and how that capital is divided into a fixed amount.

capital gains tax. A tax on chargeable gains arising on the disposal of assets over the limit for exemption.

capital goods. Certain specified plant or machinery may be relieved from VAT as capital goods.

capital redemption reserve fund. A fund which must be established by a company out of undistributed profits where redeemable preference shares (**q.v.**) are redeemed from sources other than a fresh issue.

capital reserve. That part of the reserve (**q.v.**) held back by a limited company, which may not be distributed in due course.

capitalisation of profits. The conversion of a company's profits to capital instead of paying them as dividends. This may be achieved by the issue of bonus shares or the discharge of shareholders' liability on shares not fully paid up.

captain's protest. Sworn statement by a ship's captain for insurance purposes giving full details relating to a loss.

car dealer. For VAT purposes, a taxable person (**q.v.**) who carries on a business consisting of or including the sale of motor cars.

caravans. Caravans above a certain weight limit are zero-rated for VAT (Sch. 5, VATA).

Cardiff free zone. An area of Cardiff has been designated as a free zone (**q.v.**) for the purposes of duty and VAT.

care. The provision of care in a hospital or other approved institution is exempt from VAT (Sch. 6, VATA).

care and management. The placing of a tax or duty under the care and management of the Commissioners of Customs and Excise renders it an assigned matter (**q.v.**).

cargo book. A book to be kept by the master of every coasting ship into which details required by Customs and Excise must be entered.

cargo lien. A charge which may be levied against the cargo in respect of special services.

carnet. A document replacing normal customs documentation for certain temporary importations and exportations.

carriage paid. A contract under which the vendor arranges and pays for transport of goods cleared for export to an agreed destination.

cartel. An agreement between business organisations independent of each other to share the market between them.

case. In relation to dutiable alcoholic liquor, 1 dozen units of a container holding not less than 65 nor more than 80 centilitres, or the equivalent.

cash accounting. A scheme for the accounting and payment of VAT on the basis of cash paid and received.

cash bingo. Bingo where the prizes are cash.

cash with order. A term of a contract and offer indicating that if payment is not made with the order accepting the offer, then the goods will not be sent.

caveat emptor. The principle that a buyer should take care to watch out for any defects, implying that he should bear the consequences of any which he fails to notice.

CCCN. The Nomenclature of the Customs Co-operation Council (**q.v.**). Previously the basis of the Tariff (**q.v.**).

ceiling. Machinery for limiting the amount of preference goods (**q.v.**) imported into the European Community.

Central Criminal Court. The senior criminal court for Greater London, familiarly known as the Old Bailey.

certificate of age. A customs certification of the period for which certain spirits for export have been stored in wood and in bond in the United Kingdom.

certificate of incorporation. The document issued by the Registrar of Companies evidencing that all formalities of registration have been complied with.

certificate of insolvency. A certificate issued by an administrative receiver in connection with a claim for bad debt relief which is based on insolvency.

certificate of origin. A certification in a prescribed form stating the country in which imported goods were grown, produced or manufactured.

certificate of pratique. A pass issued by customs allowing a ship arriving from abroad to proceed to her berth in port.

certificate of registry. The document issued by a Registrar on the completion of the registration of a British ship.

certificate of survey. A certificate issued after the surveying of a ship containing the particulars required to be entered on the registration of a British ship.

certiorari. An order of the High Court to review proceedings where there is a suggestion of bias, excess of jurisdiction, or an error on the record.

cesser clause. A clause in a contract for the carriage of goods by sea providing for the ending of the charterer's liability when the goods are loaded onto the ship.

cession. In international law, a method of transferring territory from one state to another.

cesspool. The emptying of cesspools is zero-rated for VAT as a sewerage service (Sch. 5, VATA).

cestui que trust. One on whose behalf property is held or administered by another person bound in conscience; a beneficiary.

chairman of ways and means. The ex-officio chairman of all committees of the House of Commons, who also acts as Deputy Speaker.

challenge for cause. An objection by the defence to a particular juror with the reason being stated.

challenge to the array. An objection by the defence to all the jurors who have been empanelled.

challenge to the polls. An objection by the defence to a particular juror.

challenge without cause. An objection by the defence to a particular juror without the reason being stated.

chambers. (1) A set of offices from which barristers work. (2) The venue for private hearings by judges not taken in open court.

Chancellor of the Exchequer. The minister who is political chief of the Treasury (**q.v.**) and responsible for control of national expenditure.

change of rate. Modified VAT rules may be applied in the case of supplies which span a change of rate.

Channel Committee (chancomtee). An organisation the members of which may be entitled to personal relief (**q.v.**) from duty and tax on importation.

Channel Islands. The islands of Guernsey, Jersey, Aldeney, Sark and their respective dependencies.

charge. A liability in respect of the property of a person or company, for example by making it the security for a loan by way of mortgage.

chargeable assets. In a transfer of a going concern, the assets of a business which are transferred, and accordingly not treated as a taxable supply.

charges clause. A provision in a contractual document setting out who is to bear the cost of specified items.

charitable trust. A public trust for the relief of poverty, the advancement of religion, the advancement of education, or any other purpose beneficial to the community.

charity. Certain supplies made by a charity are zero-rated for VAT (Sch. 5, VATA). Certain articles imported in connection with charity may be relieved from VAT.

charter commission. The amount to be paid by a shipowner to a broker who has obtained a charter for it.

charterer. A person making a contract with a shipowner for the carriage of goods by sea (charterparty).

charterparty. A contract by which a shipowner agrees to place his vessel at the disposal of another person (charterer) for the carriage of goods by sea.

charts. Charts are zero-rated for VAT (Sch. 5, VATA).

chattels real. Leaseholds.

cheating the Revenue. A criminal offence still existing at common law, which Customs and Excise may use in duty or VAT prosecutions.

chemin de fer. A game in respect of which gaming licence duty is payable for any premises on which it is played.

cheque . A bill of exchange (**q.v.**) which requires a banker to pay on demand.

cheque card. A device to increase the acceptability of cheques by backing it up to a certain amount with the credit of the issuing bank.

cheque payable to order. A cheque which can only be negotiated by signature and delivery.

chicory. Zero-rated for VAT as food of a kind used for human consumption (Sch. 5, VATA).

chief. An enhanced computerised system for Customs Handling of Import and Export Freight.

chief registrar of shipping. The holder for the time being of the office of Collector of Customs and Excise, London Port.

children's picture books. Children's picture books are zero-rated for VAT (Sch. 5, VATA).

chuck a luck. A game in respect of which gaming licence duty is payable for any premises on which it is played.

cider. A liquor less than 8.5% in strength made from the fermentation of apple juice.

C.I.F. (cost, insurance, freight). A contract by which a seller agrees to deliver goods on board a ship for a particular destination, meet freight and insurance charges, and take out at his expense a policy of marine insurance against the risks of the voyage.

C.I.F.&E. A contract by which the seller bears costs of insurance and freight, and in addition the risk of exchange fluctuations.

C.I.F.I. cost, insurance, freight and interest. A type of contract in which in addition to freight and insurance, interest is also added to the value of the shipment.

circuit judge. The rank of judicial officer presiding in crown courts and county courts.

circulating capital. That part of the property of a company which has been acquired or brought into existence in order to dispose of it, hopefully for profit.

circumstantial evidence. Facts put forward as a means of proving an allegation by deduction rather than direct evidence.

citizen's arrest. One of a limited number of situations where a member of the public can make an arrest without warrant.

civil fraud. A term popularly applied in VAT to the civil penalty of conduct involving dishonesty.

claimant. In relation to proceedings for the condemnation of goods, anyone claiming that the goods are not liable to forfeiture.

classification. The act of deciding the correct class or code in the Tariff (**q.v.**), which is appropriate to particular goods.

clawback. A charge payable to IBAP (q.v. intervention board for agricultural produce) by exporters of sheep and sheepmeat and goats and goatmeat. It is equivalent to the variable slaughter premium payable in the week of export.

clean bill of health. A certificate that a ship left a particular port at a time when there was no infectious disease there.

clean bill of lading. A bill of lading (**q.v.**) containing no qualification about the condition of the goods or their packing.

clearance inwards. The clearance from customs requirements of arrivals from abroad.

clearance outwards. Customs authority for departure from a place in the United Kingdom for a destination abroad.

clearing bank. One of the main national banks which form an association of clearing houses which exchange and settle orders for payment drawn on them.

close company. A company controlled by five or fewer people.

clothing. Articles designed as clothing for young children and not suitable for older persons are zero-rated for VAT (Sch. 5, VATA).

CMR Convention. The Convention on the Contract for the International Carriage of Goods by Road 1956.

CMR Note. An international consignment note required under the CMR Convention (**q.v.**).

club registration. The separate registration for VAT of a club, as distinct from its members.

coal. Zero-rated for VAT when held out for sale solely as fuel (Sch. 5, VATA).

coal gas. Zero-rated for VAT as fuel and power (Sch. 5, VATA).

coastguard. Originally a customs staff formed in 1822 by amalgamating the Preventative Waterguard, Revenue Cruisers and Riding Officers. Management was transferred to the Admiralty in 1856, and to the Board of Trade in 1925.

coasting trade. Trade by sea between two ports in the United Kingdom.

coasting ship. Any ship for the time being engaged in carrying goods coastwise between places in the United Kingdom (including the Isle of Man).

cocoa. Zero-rated for VAT as food of a kind used for human consumption (Sch. 5, VATA).

codes. Additional instruments to the General Agreement on Tariffs and Trade (**q.v.**), open for signature by any member, and covering mainly non-tariff measures.

codified. Applied to one act of Parliament which has drawn together all previous law on a subject; also used in Britain to distinguish foreign legal systems based entirely on written laws.

codifying statute. An act of Parliament which gathers together all existing law on a particular subject, both in other acts and in cases so as to present it as a complete body of law.

coercion. A defence sometimes raised in criminal cases, rarely successfully, on the basis that the person accused was forced to act as he did.

coffee. Zero-rated for VAT as food of a kind used for human consumption (Sch. 5, VATA).

coke. Zero-rated for VAT when held out for sale solely as fuel (Sch. 5, VATA).

collection. One of the geographical units into which the United Kingdom is divided for purposes of customs and excise, and headed by a Collector (**q.v.**).

Collection Investigation Unit (CIU). A local team of specialised Customs and Excise investigators located within each collection (**q.v.**).

Collector of Customs and Excise. The controller of a regional division, and the highest local rank in the Department of Customs and Excise.

collectors' pieces. Supplies of collectors' pieces are subject to a margin scheme (**q.v.**), and only subject to VAT on the difference between acquisition and disposal prices.

colour index. For hydrocarbon oil duty (**q.v.**), an index compiled by the Society of Dyers and Colonists, and the American Association of Textile Chemists and Colonists.

combined nomenclature. The combined tariff and statistical nomenclatures of the European Community.

Comecon. The Communist block equivalent in Eastern Europe of the Common Market, now defunct.

commander. In relation to an aircraft, includes anyone having or taking charge or command of it.

commercial bingo club. A club operating the playing of bingo, and run commercially for profit.

commercial blockade. A technique employed by nations during hostilities, by which one closes the ports of the other to foreign trade.

commercial court. For cases in the Queen's Bench Division (**q.v.**) of specialised commercial subject matter.

commissary goods. Goods of little significance for duty purposes such as catering supplies and equipment.

commission agent. A representative who acts for an agreed commission, frequently where there is a foreign principal.

Commission for the New Towns. A body which may be entitled to a refund of VAT in certain circumstances under s. 20, VATA.

Commission of the EEC. The executive body of the Common Market, which initiates its policy, and drafts proposals to carry it out.

Commissioner of Customs and Excise. A member of the Board of Customs and Excise.

Commissioner of Inland Revenue. A member of the Board of Inland Revenue.

Commissioners. Frequently applied to the Commissioners of Customs and Excise (**q.v.**), and is so defined for VAT purposes.

committal order. An order committing a person to prison for contempt of court.

committal proceedings. A hearing before magistrates to establish whether there is sufficient evidence of a serious crime to justify a trial by jury.

committee of public accounts. A committee of MPs of all parties which examines the appropriation accounts (**q.v.**) made by the various departments of state.

committee stage. The clause by clause consideration of a bill by a parliamentary committee.

commodity code. In the Tariff (**q.v.**), the code identifying a line of nomenclature.

Common Agricultural Policy (CAP). A corner-stone of the Common Market, aiming to stabilise food prices, and guarantee the income of food producers.

common assault. The offence of using or threatening force against another person.

common carrier. A person undertaking to carry the person or goods of anyone who chooses to employ him from one place to another in return for payment.

Common Council of the City of London. A body which as a local authority may be entitled to a refund of VAT in certain circumstances under s. 20, VATA.

Common Customs Tariff. The published authority of the European Community for its tariff and trade statistical nomenclature. In case of conflict, it prevails over Customs and Excise Integrated Tariff of the United Kingdom. ('The Tariff' q.v.).

common law. Strictly, the general law contained in decided cases, as opposed to acts of Parliament, but also used to include law in acts of Parliament with decided cases as a contrast with Equity (**q.v.**). A third use is to distinguish the English (common-law) system from a foreign system of law.

common law cheat. An ancient criminal offence covering a wide range of deceptions which has now been largely replaced by modern statutory offences. Cheating the public revenue however, remains.

common law corporation. Created by express or presumed charter of the Monarch, such as corporations of the City of London.

Common Market Law Reports. A series of published decisions in cases relating to matters of EEC interest.

common seal. The mark of corporate personality, which every registered limited company had to possess, with its name legibly engraved thereon. Since 31 July 1990, a company need not have a common seal.

Common Serjeant. A senior barrister exercising special judicial functions in the Central Criminal Court (Old Bailey), and also the Mayor's and City of London Court.

common stocking. The storage of inward-processing relief (**q.v.**) goods and non-inward processing relief goods without distinction.

common transit. Community transit (**q.v.**) by and in relation to the EFTA (**q.v.**) countries.

Commonwealth. A loose and informal association of nations and territories having some link with the United Kingdom and acknowledging its sovereign as Head of Commonwealth.

community carnet. A document acting as the import and export declaration covering certain goods being taken or sent to another European Community country for temporary use and return.

community council. In Wales, a body which may be entitled to a refund of VAT in certain circumstances under s. 20, VATA.

community customs duty. An expression which includes any agricultural levy, tax or charge under the common agricultural policy, (**q.v.**) or under any special arrangements applicable to goods resulting from the processing of agricultural products.

community goods. Goods which originate in or which are in free circulation (**q.v.**) in the European Community (**q.v.**).

community resources. The income funding the Common Market, derived from import duties and levies and national value added tax.

community service order. A punishment imposed by a criminal court whereby the person sentenced must attend a particular place to carry out a prescribed amount of unpaid work.

community transit. A system of moving European Community goods between member states with minimal customs formalities at frontiers.

community transit document. A document for use under community transit (**q.v.**) provisions, indicating the goods covered.

community traveller. A person whose domicile, habitual residence or usual place of business is in a member state of the European Community other than the United Kingdom.

commutation. Part of the Royal Prerogative, by which a lesser punishment is substituted for a greater one. The Commissioners of Customs and Excise enjoy a similar power.

companies liquidation account. An account maintained at the Bank of England into which a liquidator is obliged to pay all money he receives during the course of the winding-up of a company.

company director. A senior commercial manager of a trading concern subject to obligations and rights under company legislation.

company member. A shareholder in a company limited by shares.

company promotion. The procedure by which a company is incorporated by registration and established as a going concern.

company secretary. An officer who must be engaged by every limited company, and a position which cannot be filled by a sole director.

compellability. The condition of a witness being obliged to give evidence.

compensating products. Goods which have been exported from the United Kingdom in another form, and which, after processing abroad, have been returned to the United Kingdom.

compensation for loss of office. Compensation paid to the directors of a company who lose their positions following a change in its control.

compensation order. A court order made against a convicted criminal directing him to make amends to the person affected by his crime.

compensatory amount. A charge which may be made in the oils and fats sector of the Common Agricultural Policy (**q.v.**).

compensatory levy. A system to equalise rates of duty between established members of the European Community and newly admitted members during a transitional period.

completion. A formal meeting between solicitors for the purchasers and vendors of property to hand over the purchase money and tie up the last formalities.

composite invoice. An invoice which may be issued for VAT purposes where continuous supplies of services are made and successive payments arise.

composition with creditors. An arrangement or settlement arrived at between a debtor and his creditors after bankruptcy proceedings have been started.

compounder. A person holding an excise licence to compound spirits.

COMPRO. A European association of state sponsored bodies which aim to simplify international trade procedures.

Comptroller and Auditor-General. An official appointed by the Crown to examine accounts of income and expenditure made by the various departments of state.

compulsory winding-up. A dissolution of a company brought about by order of the court.

concurrent sentence. A sentence of imprisonment expressed to run at the same time as a sentence for another offence, so that no additional time is served.

condenser. A heat exchanger condensing vapourised alcohol into its liquid form, and collected via the low wines or spirits safe.

condemnation. The forfeiture of an article by due process of law, after it has been lawfully seized by an authorised person.

condition. An element in a contract of such fundamental importance that the agreement may fail if it is not carried out.

condition precedent. An event which must take place before a particular agreement can be carried out.

condition subsequent. A future event which may affect an agreement previously entered into.

conditional bill of sale. A bill of sale (**q.v.**) giving a claim over the goods or security for the payment of money which ceases to have effect on repayment of the money.

conditional bond. A personal security for the payment of money or the carrying out of some other act, with a condition that it will become void if the act is completed within a certain time.

conditional discharge. An order made by a court in a criminal case, whereby no immediate punishment is imposed on the person discharged.

conditional sale. Certain conditional sale agreements are exempt from VAT (Sch. 6, VATA).

conduct involving dishonesty. An ingredient of the civil penalty in VAT popularly known as 'civil fraud'.

confectionery. Certain confectionery does not qualify for zero-rating for VATA (Sch. 5, VATA).

confirmed letter of credit. An arrangement between a bank and its customer who has bought goods that payment will be made to the seller on presentation of certain documents of authority.

confirming house. An organisation based in an exporter's country which procures and pays for goods on behalf of the client overseas.

competency. In relation to a witness, the state of being able to give admissible evidence.

consecutive sentence. A sentence of imprisonment expressed to run after a sentence imposed for another offence, so that the two terms are added together.

consideration. The price or value by which one person obtains an undertaking in contract from another person.

consignor. In international trade, the last owner from whom imported goods were procured.

consignee. In international trade, the person who receives goods.

consolidated fund. Constituted in 1787 by combining the duties of Customs, Excise, Stamps and Post Office, and pledged for payment of the consolidated national debt of the United Kingdom.

consolidating statute. A statute which collects together all existing statutes on a particular subject without altering or amending any of the provisions in those statutes.

consolidation. The joining up of a number of legal issues which are in the course of proceedings in the same court.

consortium. A pooling of effort by two or more business enterprises to achieve a particular objective, which will end when that objective is achieved.

conspiracy. (1) A civil action in respect of the combination of people with the intention of causing damage to another, and which results in damage. (2) The agreement of two or more people to commit a criminal offence.

constable. Prior to the establishment of the police force, an official appointed in every parish to keep the peace. Used in customs legislation to describe a member of the police force.

control visit. A visit by a VAT officer to a taxable person (**q.v.**) to check his VAT records and books.

construction of dwellings. Certain grants of major interests by persons constructing dwellings may be zero-rated for VAT (Sch. 5, VATA).

constructive loss. The situation where the subject-matter of an insurance policy is justifiably abandoned, either because its destruction seems inevitable, or the cost of repair would be too great.

constructive trust. A form of trust arising where a trustee performs an act in his own name in respect of property held by him as a trustee.

constructive warehousing. The formal recording of particulars of dutiable goods in a bonded warehouse without physically depositing them there.

consular invoice. A certificate given by a consul as to local prices and shipping charges for the purposes of import duties.

consultant. The supply of services of a consultant are treated as supplied where received for VAT purposes.

consumer protection advisory committee. A body created to advance the interests of fair trading by considering whether any practice referred to it adversely affects a consumer's interests.

container. Large returnable transport units specially designed for the carriage of freight. Includes any bundle or package and any box, cask or receptacle.

contango. The act of postponing payment for shares from one settlement period until another.

contemnor. A person who has committed a contempt of court (**q.v.**).

contempt of court. Disobedience of a court order made in a civil case, or an act interfering with the course of justice.

continental shelf. Much used in international and maritime law, it refers to the land area under the sea off the coast of a country, which extends in ledge form before eventually coming to deep seas.

continuation clause. A clause in a policy of marine insurance automatically extending cover for 30 days or until the ship's safe arrival, whichever is the earlier.

continuing guarantee. An arrangement by which the liability of the guarantor (**q.v.**) is spread over a number of transactions covering a period of time.

contract. A legally binding agreement under which one side promises to do or not to do certain things at the request of the other side, or for its benefit.

contract of record. The entry of a debt on the official record of a court of record (**q.v.**), having the effect of a judgment imposed on an individual.

contract of service. A contract of employment between master and servant (employer and employee).

contract for services. A contract for work to be carried out by an independent contractor (**q.v.**), as opposed to a contract of service or employment.

contract under seal. A contract made by deed, otherwise known as a speciality contract (**q.v.**), and therefore not needing consideration (**q.v.**).

contribution clause. A clause in a fire insurance policy providing that if any other insurance has been taken out on the same property, the insurer under the later policy is only liable for a proportion of any loss.

contributory. A past or present shareholder in a company who is liable to it in a winding up in respect of partly paid up shares.

controlled tenant. A tenant who enjoys the protection of the Rent Acts against eviction and unilateral increases in rent.

control of movement of goods. A system for controlling certain imported goods while in transit or being moved within the United Kingdom.

contraband. Any article prohibited to be imported or exported, and therefore smuggled if the prohibition is evaded.

controller. For the purposes of VAT administration, the Controller, Customs and Excise, Value Added Tax Central Unit.

convention. (1) A practice which is consistently followed, although not having the force of law. (2) An international agreement, which may have been ratified by the United Kingdom.

conversion. Any action by one person conflicting with the lawful ownership of goods by another person.

convertible debentures. Debenture capital (**q.v.**) giving the holders the right if they so desire of exchanging their debentures for shares.

conveyance. A document transferring a freehold interest in the sale of land; the acts involved in drawing up the documentation.

conviction. A finding of guilt against an accused person in a criminal case.

co-operative. A trading organisation with a membership of equality of control, distributing any profits among the members.

copyright. The right to control certain ways of dealing with a book, play, film or other creative work made the subject of protection, usually for the life of the creator, and a period after his death. For VAT purposes, it is a service supplied where received.

copyright collecting society. A body responsible for the collection and distribution of royalties arising from the use of works protected by copyright.

copyright owner. The person having the right to control any work protected by the system of copyright (**q.v.**).

copyright piracy. The unauthorised manufacture by copying of material protected by copyright, such as books, films and records. Importation of infringing copies may be prohibited.

Coreper. The Committee of Permanent Representatives of the Common Market.

corn exchange. A London market for dealing in grain and other crops for immediate as opposed to future delivery.

coroner. An official, who should be legally or medically qualified, appointed to conduct enquiries by way of inquest into sudden death and treasure trove (**q.v.**).

coroner's court. A court presided over by a coroner to conduct enquiries into cases of sudden death and treasure trove (**q.v.**).

coroner's jury. A panel of not fewer than seven and not more than eleven persons summoned to consider certain types of case where sudden death has taken place.

corporation aggregate. A body consisting of a number of individual members, existing because of a charter or act of Parliament (in particular the Companies Acts).

corporation sole. One of a number of certain offices capable of being filled only by one person at a time; e.g. the Bishop of London.

corporation tax. A tax paid by a company at a single rate on all profits, whether distributed or not.

corporeal chattels. Material things, such as goods, which can be physically touched.

cost and freight (C & F). A contract under which the seller has to pay the costs and freight necessary to bring goods to a specified destination, where risk and any cost increase transfers to the buyer when goods cross the ship's rail in the port of shipment.

costs between solicitor and own client. The most generous basis on which costs are allowed, taking account of special fees and expenses.

Council of Europe. A rather informal association of most of the former non-Communist countries in Europe, co-operating in many fields, with the eventual aim of European unity.

Council of Legal Education. The body controlling the syllabus and examinations for admission to the barrister's profession.

Council of Ministers. The decision making body of the EEC, which considers proposals put up by the Commission (**q.v.**).

Council of the Isles of Scilly. A body which as a local authority may be entitled to a refund of VAT in certain circumstances under s. 20, VATA.

Council of the Stock Exchange. The governing body of the Stock Exchange.

Council on Tribunals. The governing body which reviews the constitution and operation of administrative tribunals.

count. An allegation in an indictment (**q.v.**). More than one count may be included.

counter-claim. A cross-action brought by the defendant against the person claiming from him.

counterfeiting. The act of making a false copy, particularly in relation to currency.

counterpart. A duplicate copy of a legal document, particularly a lease.

countertrade. A contract in international trade to pay for the purchase of goods with other goods rather than money.

county council. A body which as a local authority may be entitled to a refund of VAT in certain circumstances under s. 20, VATA.

countervailing duty. A duty imposed on imports to counter the effects of export subsidies applied by an exporting country.

county court. The lowest level of court for civil disputes such as contract, negligence, and landlord and tenant. Now with extended jurisdiction.

county court judge. A member of the judiciary of circuit judge status who sits in the county court to try civil matters.

county court registrar. An official of the county court, subordinate to the judge, who performs administrative functions, and carries out some judicial duties.

country of origin. The country in which goods were produced or manufactured.

Court of Appeal (civil division). It hears appeals in civil cases from county courts, divisional courts and the High Court.

Court of Appeal (criminal division). It hears appeals from the Crown Court in criminal cases triable by jury.

court of first instance. A general term for a court in which a case is first tried, from which an appeal to a higher court may be made.

Court of Piepowder. A medieval court exclusively for merchants, settling disputes arising in their marketplaces. Probably deriving from 'pieds poudres' — dusty feet.

Court of Protection. A court which sits to administer the property of people who are of unsound mind, or under other disability.

Court of Session. The supreme court of civil jurisdiction in the Scottish legal system; not to be confused with the former English quarter sessions (**q.v.**).

Courts of the Staple. Courts of the Middle Ages dealing with the laws of merchants in the principal trading towns.

covenant. An agreement, undertaking or promise contained in a deed.

cover note. A certificate containing particulars of temporary insurance cover arranged pending the issue of a full policy.

craft clause. A provision in a contract of marine insurance relating to the ferrying of goods in a transit craft to the vessel in which they will ultimately be carried.

craps. A game in respect of which gaming licence duty is payable for premises on which it is played.

credit. The making of any advance or the granting of any credit is exempt from VAT (Sch. 6, VATA).

credit brokerage business. Any commercial concern which puts potential customers in touch with organisations prepared to lend money under consumer credit agreements (**q.v.**). It requires a licence from the Director General of Fair Trading.

credit for input tax. The machinery under which the VAT a taxable person (**q.v.**) has paid on a supply made to him or on an importation is repaid by Customs and Excise.

credit insurance company. A private organisation guaranteeing the carrying out of contracts by overseas purchasers, where credit cannot otherwise be relied on.

credit note. A document issued by a seller for an item overcharged on an earlier invoice, or where goods delivered have to be taken back by him, for example because of defect or error. In certain circumstances may be used for VAT.

credit office. Bookmaking premises to which the public are not admitted, and which do not require a betting office licence (**q.v.**).

credit sale. Certain credit sale agreements are exempt from VAT (Sch. 6, VATA).

creek. A tidal inlet which in the absence of special licence is not a lawful place of importation or exportation.

creep. In measuring hydrocarbon oil (**q.v.**), the tendency of meters to run on.

cremation. The disposal of the dead and connected arrangements is exempt from VAT (Sch. 6, VATA).

crew. In relation to a ship or aircraft, all persons actually employed in its working, including the master or commander.

crew declaration. A declaration to be made on arrival of a ship from abroad by the master and crew giving details of certain goods.

crime. A wrong against the community which is punishable by the state.

criminal bankruptcy. An order which may be made by a Crown Court on convicting someone whose offence caused loss or damage above a particular sum.

criminal fraud. In the VAT offence code, fraud tried by a criminal court as opposed to conduct involving dishonesty which attracts a civil penalty.

criminal responsibility. The age at which a person is regarded by the law as being capable of committing a criminal offence.

criminology. The scientific study of criminal motivation, its causes, effects and treatment.

crown and anchor. A game in respect of which gaming licence duty is payable for any premises on which it is played.

crown copyright. The right of the Crown to control copyright in all works made by or under government directions.

Crown Court. The senior level of criminal court which hears cases triable by jury.

Crown in Council. The reigning sovereign together with the Privy Council.

Crown prerogative. The administration of justice exercised through the courts and judges on behalf of the sovereign.

Crown Prosecuting Solicitor (CPS). A lawyer employed to conduct prosecutions for the police within the jurisdiction of a particular police authority.

crystallisation. The conversion of a floating charge (**q.v.**) over all the assets of a company into a fixed charge (**q.v.**) over certain definite assets. It takes place on the occurrence of certain events, such as a winding-up.

cumulative preference shares. A category of preference shares (**q.v.**) in a limited company where any deficiency in paying previous dividends must be made up before paying ordinary shareholders.

currency. Generally applied to forms of money issued or circulated by the governmental authority of a state, as opposed to a banker's draft.

currency code. In customs entries, a 2-alpha code which notifies the currency in which a customs value is being declared.

current account. The operation of a current account is exempt from VAT (Sch. 6, VATA).

current accounting year. The current accounting period for the purpose of the VAT annual accounting scheme.

custom. A local rule both reasonable and certain deemed to have existed since time immemorial, and accepted as part of the law of the land.

custom house. The public office at which the customs business of a port is carried out.

Customs and Excise airport. An aerodrome for the time being designated as a place for the landing or departure of aircraft for the purpose of customs and excise.

Customs and Excise station. A place appointed for the examination and entry of and payment of any duty chargeable on goods being imported or exported across the Irish land boundary.

Customs and Excise tariff. A volume prepared annually showing the duties, drawbacks and allowances of Customs and Excise.

Customs and Excise warehouse. A warehouse approved by Customs and Excise both as a customs and as an excise warehouse.

customs bond. A security demanded by Customs and Excise for goods subject to a duty, which is not for the time being to be fully paid.

Customs Co-operation Council (CCC). An inter-governmental organisation scrutinising matters relating to customs procedures in an effort to produce a measure of uniformity.

customs duty. A charge on imported goods levied under the Common Customs Tariff (**q.v.**) of the European Community, any other charges having equivalent effect, and agricultural levy.

customs entry. A document in prescribed form giving particulars of goods from abroad which an importer wishes to pass through customs. See new Single Administrative Document (SAD).

customs input of entry. The input of an entry into the customs entry processing system by customs itself, as opposed to direct trader input (**q.v.**).

customs procedure code. A code which identifies the customs and/or excise regimes to which goods are being entered, and from which (if applicable) they have been removed.

customs registered number. A unique five digit number assigned to an exporter or an agent who has received Customs and Excise approval to use certain specified export procedures.

customs seals. Seals which customs officers apply to secure goods under customs control.

customs territory of the community. The single customs area to which European Community legislation expressly refers, especially in the field of customs.

customs union. A union of two or more countries within which customs duties are progressively removed and a common external tariff erected against non-members. The Common Market (European Economic Community q.v.) is an example.

customs value. The value of imported goods for customs purposes.

customs warehouse. A warehouse approved by Customs and Excise for the deposit of imported goods liable to customs duty or otherwise not in free circulation.

D

damages. An award made by way of compensation to the aggrieved party in a civil action.

dandy note. A document used in the Port of London to notify the delivery to the side of an exporting ship of goods from warehouse.

dangerous drug. A drug which, if listed in the relevant legislation, is subject to a prohibition on importation.

dangerous goods shipping note. A standardised document for the delivery of hazardous cargo to port areas and container bases in the United Kingdom.

datapost packet. A postal packet containing goods posted in the United Kingdom for transmission abroad, or received in the United Kingdom from abroad for transmission and delivery as a datapost packet.

date of commencement. The date on which an act of Parliament or statutory instrument (**q.v.**) comes into effect.

day rate of levy. The rate of levy fixed by European Community Regulations which is in operation on a particular day.

dead freight. The sum due to a shipowner who is ready to fulfil a contract for the carriage of goods by sea, but the charterer has failed to load a full cargo.

dear money. Money borrowed at a high rate of interest.

debenture. Issued by a limited company in respect of a loan generally secured on its assets. By contrast with debenture stock (**q.v.**) it constitutes an individual debt between company and debenture holder. The issue, transfer, receipt or dealing with debentures is exempt from VAT (Sch. 6, VATA).

debenture capital. Money borrowed on the security of the issue of debentures (**q.v.**) or debenture stock (**q.v.**), which is in effect a loan to a limited company against the security of its assets.

debit note. An additional invoice to cover an omission or undercharging on a previous invoice.

de bonis non administratis. Property left without administration.

de jure. As a matter of law.

debt. An ancient form of action by which a claim for money alleged to be owed could be made.

debt collecting business. Any organisation which collects debts arising under consumer credit agreements, which must be licensed by the Director-General of Fair Trading.

debt counselling business. Any concern advising clients on the liquidation of debts or negotiating settlements under consumer credit agreements. It must be licensed by the Director-General of Fair Trading.

debt due to the Crown. VAT due to Customs and Excise from any person is recoverable as a debt due to the Crown.

deck cargo. Cargo or stores carried in any uncovered space on the deck of a ship or other covered space not forming part of the ship's registered tonnage.

declarant. A person who signs a customs entry, or valuation statement, or who makes a statement of a similar nature relating to customs.

declaration for relief. The act by which a person applies for relief from duty on the importation of goods.

declaration of association. A statement in the memorandum of association of a company that the subscribers wish to form a company, and that they agree to take the prescribed shares.

deed of arrangement. A procedure by which a person in financial difficulties can put his property in trust for the benefit of his creditors, without actually becoming bankrupt.

default surcharge. A civil penalty imposed on a person who makes a specified number of defaults in his VAT affairs in a given period of time.

defeasance. Any collateral agreement relating to a bill of sale (**q.v.**) which allows the bill to be set aside if events mentioned in the agreement take place.

defendant. In criminal law, a person subject to a criminal action, in civil law, a person against whom an action is brought.

deferment approval number (DAN). A number allocated by Customs and Excise to traders who are approved to defer payment of customs charges.

deferred annuity. A policy by which payment of a stated annual sum, the annuity, is delayed for a specific number of years after the making of the contract.

deferred creditor. A creditor who has a low priority in participating in the division of any assets of a bankrupt.

deferred payment. A system for the deferment of customs duties payable on imported goods, agricultural levies (**q.v.**), and VAT payable on imported goods.

deferred shares. A category of shares which may exist in the structure of a company, providing their holders with entitlement to all the remaining profit after the ordinary shareholders have received a fixed dividend.

degressivity. The principle that a measure restricting or distorting trade should be phased out over a period of time.

del credere agent. An agent who assumes responsibility for the accounts of his customers, and indemnifies his principal against losses caused by any customers introduced by him.

delegated legislation. Orders, regulations and rules having the force of an act of Parliament, but made by somebody outside Parliament to whom the power to make them has been deputed by Parliament.

delivered at frontier (DAF). A contract under which the vendor assumes responsibility until the goods reach the frontier in the country of destination.

delivered domicile. A contract by which the seller must arrange and pay all charges for delivering goods to the buyer's premises.

delivered duty paid (DDP). A contract in which the seller undertakes to deliver generally at specified premises goods on which import duties have been paid.

delivered duty unpaid (DDU). A contract under which the vendor assumes the risk and expense of getting goods to a stated destination exclusive of duty, taxes and charges on importation.

delivered ex ship (DES). A contract under which the vendor is responsible for goods until unloading at the port of destination.

delivery order. An order made by the owner of goods, allowing the person who has charge of them to hand them over to a specified person.

demise charter. An agreement for the charter of a ship only, without its crew.

demurrage. Money payable by charterers to a shipowner for delay to a vessel due to her being kept beyond an agreed or reasonable period for loading or discharge.

denaturing. The act of making a commodity unfit for human consumption by adding something to it.

dental auxiliary. The supply of services by a person enrolled on any roll of dental auxiliaries is exempt from VAT (Sch. 6, VATA).

dental technician. The supply of services by a dental technician is exempt from VAT (Sch. 6, VATA).

dentist. The supply of services by a person on the register of dentists is exempt from VAT (Sch. 6, VATA).

departmental entry processing system (DEPS). The computerised system used by Customs and Excise for processing import entries.

department of state. An organ of central government headed by a minister, popularly known as a ministry. An example is the Department of the Environment. Another is Customs and Excise.

Department of Trade Inspector. A person who may be appointed by the Department of Trade to investigate the affairs of a company where there is a suggestion of serious mismanagement.

dependant. For customs purposes, an entitled person's spouse, or any other person wholly or mainly maintained by him, or in his custody, charge or care.

deponent. Someone who makes a statement on oath.

deportation order. An order requiring a person of non-UK nationality to leave the United Kingdom, and to remain out of the country.

deposit account. The operation of a deposit account is exempt from VAT (Sch. 6, VATA).

deposition. Oral statement of evidence taken down before magistrates at old-style committal proceedings (**q.v.**).

derelict. An abandoned vessel still afloat.

derogation. The act of prejudicing, evading or completely destroying some entitlement or grant. It is particularly applied to the law of the European Community.

derv. Fuel for Diesel Engined Road Vehicles. A heavy oil attracting a higher rate of excise duty.

designation order. An order designating an area of the United Kingdom as a free zone for customs purposes.

derogation. A departure from prescribed procedure, in particular, a departure in the domestic law of a member state from a rule laid down in European Community law.

deterrent sentence. A high sentence passed by a judge who has a choice of options, in order to make an example of the person he is sentencing.

devaluation. The lowering of the value of one state's currency against the currencies of other states.

development corporation. A body entitled to a refund of VAT in certain circumstances under s. 20, VATA.

deviation. For purposes of marine insurance, the departure of a ship from a standard or agreed course of navigation.

diligence. (1) A type of action for recovery in Scotland, used by Customs and Excise in connection with VAT arrears. (2) Forms of summary recovery exercisable in Scotland, and used in respect of VAT debts.

Dillon Round. The 5th round of multilateral trade negotiations of GATT (**q.v.**), which took place in 1961/2.

diplomatic immunity. The immunity from both civil and criminal proceedings granted to foreign ambassadors and certain categories of their staff.

dipping rod. A rod for measuring quantities of liquid subject to customs control.

directive. An ordinance of the Council of Ministers (**q.v.**) of the Common Market, binding on member countries as to the result to be achieved.

directly applicable legislation. Laws made by the Common Market, in particular directives which take effect directly in this country, and do not need to be passed through Parliament.

Director of Public Prosecutions. A senior appointment in the government legal service heading his own department of lawyers. He advises certain other government departments, also the police in certain classes of case, and prosecutes in cases of particular difficulty or magnitude.

directors' report. A statement which must be attached each year to a company's balance sheet, relating to the company's dividends and affairs.

direct trader input. An arrangement under which traders key customs declarations direct to the Customs and Excise entry processing system.

direct trader input port. A port with the facility for computerising import entries directly made by the importer.

disaggregation. The attempt to divide business activities into independent parts, so that VAT registration can be avoided. Customs and Excise counter this with anti-avoidance legislation.

discharge. The situation where the person who has made a promise in a contract becomes no longer bound by it.

discount market. Collectively, those undertakings whose main business is dealing in sterling bills.

discounting bills. The purchase of bills of exchange at their face value minus any interest remaining for the period before they mature.

disgorging. The act of removing sediment from effervescing wines in bottle.

dishonour. Where a cheque is drawn on a particular bank, which declines to pay under it, that cheque is said to be dishonoured.

dispensing optician. The supply of services by a person on the register of dispensing opticians is exempt from VAT (Sch. 6, VATA).

disputed decision. A decision of the Commissioners (**q.v.**) against which an appellant brings an appeal to a VAT Tribunal.

dispute settlement. Arrangement under GATT (**q.v.**) by which one member state can seek consultation, conciliation and independent review of measures taken by another member state.

distillation test. The operation of measuring the original gravity of wash (**q.v.**) or beer, or the alcoholic strength of wine and spirits by distillation.

distiller. A person holding an excise licence to distil spirits.

distiller's licence. An excise licence for the manufacture or distillation of spirits.

distiller's warehouse. An excise warehouse approved by Customs and Excise for the storage of spirits immediately following production in the associated distillery.

distillery. Premises where spirits are manufactured, whether by distillation of a fermented liquor, or by any other process.

distilling materials. Materials producing wort (**q.v.**) or wash (**q.v.**) the gravity of which can be ascertained by a saccharometer (**q.v.**).

distress. The process of distraining.

district council. A body which as a local authority may be entitled to a refund of VAT in certain circumstances under s. 20, VATA.

district registrar. A judicial officer supervising a district registry (**q.v.**) who decides interim issues and disputes arising during the course of legal proceedings.

district registry. A branch office of the Central Office of the Supreme Court.

distringas. The authority to distrain (**q.v.**) in execution of a court order.

divisional court. Formed in the Queen's Bench, Chancery and Family Divisions of the High Court to hear appeals from lower courts and tribunals.

divisional registration. The registration for VAT of a division of a body corporate which carries on business in several divisions.

dockage. Berthing dues payable by a vessel which has used dock accommodation while taking in cargo.

dock warrant. A warrant issued by a harbour authority allowing a particular person to take possession of goods.

documentary bill. A bill of exchange attached to the bill of lading, insurance policy and invoice for the goods it is connected with in case the bill is dishonoured.

do-it-yourself builder. A builder who may be entitled to a refund of VAT in respect of construction work, to eliminate tax distortion.

domestic bingo. Bingo played in private on domestic occasions.

domicile. The country in which an individual is considered to be permanently resident because of his connection with it.

domicile or habitual residence. The place so named in a person's passport, identity card or other identity document recognised as valid in the United Kingdom.

dominant tenement. Land benefiting from an easement or profit a prendre.

double insurance. Over-insurance by taking out two or more policies in respect of the same risk, in excess of the total to be indemnified.

doublings. Spirits of the second extraction.

drained cherries. Zero-rated for VAT as food of a kind used for human consumption (Sch. 5, VATA).

dramming. An allowance of duty-free spirit for consumption given by distillers to their workmen under the supervision of the Distillery Officer until 1899, when it was forbidden.

draught of a ship. The depth of water necessary to float a ship.

drawback. The repayment of duty on goods when they are exported, shipped as stores, or deposited in a bonded warehouse under certain conditions.

drawback of goods. Goods in the case of which a claim for drawback (**q.v.**) has been or is to be made.

drawee. The person on whom a call to pay is made by a written instrument, for example a bank.

drawer. A person who has drafted or written something out, often used in the context of cheques and other negotiable instruments.

drip. The measured quantity of liquid sufficient to cover the bottom of a gauged vessel and any curved junction.

droits of admiralty. Goods afloat at sea within the low water mark which have not become wreck (**q.v.**) by touching bottom.

drugs. The dispensing by a pharmacist of drugs prescribed by a doctor is zero-rated for VAT (Sch. 5, VATA).

DTI (DOTI). The Department of Trade and Industry.

dumping. The exporting of a product at a price which is below the cost of production, or the price on the home market, or otherwise unfairly subsidised.

duress. Pressure brought to bear to influence a person's decision.

dutiable alcoholic liquor. Applies to spirits, beer, wine, made-wine or cider, or any of these collectively.

dutiable goods. Goods of a class or description subject to any duty of customs or excise, whether or not paid.

duty deferment. A system for deferring customs and excise charges due on imports and certain home-produced and home-manufactured goods.

duty-paid goods. Goods in respect of which the Commissioners of Customs and Excise are satisfied that all relevant duties have been paid.

dynamic slip. In measuring hydrocarbon oil (**q.v.**), meters tend to under record at very low or very high flow rates.

E

E&OE. Errors and omissions excepted. A reservation of the right generally on an invoice, to correct later any errors or omissions which may become apparent.

easement. The right to make limited use of another person's land, as in a right of way.

earnings arrestment. A form of diligence (**q.v.**) used in Scotland for the recovery by Customs and Excise of unpaid VAT debts.

East India Company. Chartered in 1660 with exclusive trading rights in all places east of a line from the Cape of Good Hope to the Straits of Magellan.

Economic and Social Committee (ESC). A body established under the European Community and Euratom Treaties which considers and expresses opinions on Commission proposals to the Council.

Economic Commission for Europe. One of the regional economic commissions established by the United Nations to supervise a variety of social and economic matters.

Economic and Social Committee of the EEC. A consultative body of the Common Market, which considers proposals suggested by the Commission (**q.v.**) and the Council of Ministers (**q.v.**).

Economic and Social Council of the UN. A committee of the General Assembly of the United Nations (**q.v.**) responsible for the promotion of economic and social progress.

economic regulator. A special surcharge or rebate which may be imposed on certain customs and excise duties to regulate the balance between demand and resources in the United Kingdom.

education. Certain types of education are exempt from VAT (Sch. 6, VATA).

educational visit. A visit made by a VAT officer to a taxable person (**q.v.**) newly registered for VAT to explain the principles of the system.

effective date of registration. The date on a taxable person's certificate of registration, with effect from which he is obliged to account for VAT.

electricity. Electricity is zero-rated for VAT as fuel and power (Sch. 5, VATA).

embezzlement. A former crime involving obtaining by fraud, now replaced by the law relating to theft (**q.v.**).

enabling clause. A provision of the GATT (**q.v.**) sanctioning Generalised System of Preferences schemes (GSP q.v.).

end use. A system which allows goods to be imported at a favourable rate of duty, provided that they are put to a prescribed use under the control of Customs and Excise.

end use goods. Goods in relation to which the import duties chargeable depend on the use to be made of them.

end use relief. The relief from duty available to those importers who have availed themselves of the system of end use (**q.v.**).

endorsement. Signature, often in the context of making a transfer.

endowment assurance policy. A policy of assurance (**q.v.**) by which it is agreed that payment will be made either after expiry of a fixed term, or on the death of the life assured if earlier.

enforcement of judgment. The means of obtaining payment from a person against whom a court order has been made.

engineer. The supply of the services of an engineer is treated as supplied where received for VAT purposes.

engrossment. The preparation of a formal legal document in its final form, ready for completion by swearing, signing or other formality.

enlargement of time. An extension of a time limit.

entry for trial. The procedure whereby the person making a claim must set it down for trial, or risk it being dismissed for want of prosecution.

entry of appearance. The official notice given by a person against whom a civil claim has been made that he intends to defend the matter.

entry processing point (EPP). A Customs and Excise office which partially processes entries, but which does not have the full facilities of an entry processing unit (**q.v.**).

entry processing unit (EPU). A Customs and Excise office for the receipt and handling of import and ex-customs warehouse documentation.

equitable execution. A form of action to enforce a court order where the judgment debtor has property or interests which cannot be reached by normal legal processes.

equitable interest. A supplementary form of right developed by the Chancellor's system of equity (**q.v.**). Though weaker than a legal right developed from the common law, it supplements that system. (e.g. a trust).

equitable lien. A right over property bestowed by law on someone who is not the true owner of the property. An example would be an unpaid seller of land who had transferred legal title to the purchaser.

equitable mortgage. The tendering of land as security for a loan, so that an equitable interest in that land is established in favour of the lender.

equitable mortgage of shares. The deposit of share certificates with a lender as security for a loan, creating merely an equitable title without transfer or registration.

equity share capital. The section of the issued capital (**q.v.**) of a limited company, which places no restrictions on the holders to participate in dividends or capital.

established civil servant. A person serving in an established capacity in the permanent service of the Crown.

estimate. An offer, generally in writing, to carry out certain work at a stated price.

estimates of expenditure. Annual estimates of expenditure prepared for the Treasury by the ministers responsible for the armed forces and the civil service.

estimation. The Commissioners (**q.v.**) may in certain circumstances allow a person to estimate his VAT in a particular period.

estoppel. A rule of evidence that a person cannot deny the existence of a state of affairs which he has himself brought about, and on the basis of which another person has acted. Customs contend that estoppel does not bind the Crown.

estoppel by conduct. The condition by which a person who has led another person to believe that a particular situation exists is not able to escape the consequences of his conduct. Customs contend that estoppel does not bind the Crown.

equivalence. Relief from duty by the use of non-inward processing relief goods to produce exports, releasing inward processing relief goods for other purposes without paying duty.

esturial traffic. Water trade within defined limits of the Thames, Mersey, Clyde, Forth, Tyne and Humber deemed not to be trade by sea.

eurocrat. An international civil servant employed by one of the institutions of the Common Market.

eurodollars. Dollar balances held in European banks by companies or individual account holders.

European Agricultural Guidance and Guarantee Fund (EAGGF). The body which finances the Common Agricultural Policy of the European Community (**q.v.**).

European Atomic Energy Community. One of the organisations making up the European Economic Community, or Common Market. It is known shortly as EURATOM.

European Coal and Steel Community (ECSC). One of the organisations comprising the European Community, or Common Market.

European Court of Human Rights. The forum for the European Convention of Human Rights, to be distinguished from the European Court of Justice (**q.v.**).

European Court of Justice. The legal forum of the Common Market which is the final interpreter of EEC legislation.

European currency unit (ECU). A financial unit used for European Community accounting and intended as a valid medium of exchange.

European development fund. The means by which the Common Market's scheme of assistance for less developed countries is put into effect.

European Economic Community. The EEC, or Common Market, established by the Treaty of Rome (**q.v.**).

European Free Trade Area (**EFTA**). An association of Austria, Iceland, Norway, Portugal, Sweden and Switzerland to promote free trade in industrial products. The United Kingdom left in 1972 on joining the Common Market which itself has free-trade agreements with the EFTA states.

European Investment Bank. An organ of the Common Market arranging financial assistance for matters in which the EEC is concerned, and for certain under-developed regions.

European Monetary Co-operation Fund. A reserve fund of the central banks of the Common Market countries.

European Monetary System (**EMS**). A system under which member states of the European Community maintain their currencies within a narrow fluctuation band to obtain relative stability between their respective exchange rates.

European Parliament. An assembly of delegates from the member states of the Common Market, who sit by party to consider EEC policy.

European Space Agency. An organisation of Western European states for the co-ordination of research and execution of developments in space.

examination station. A part of an airport approved by Customs and Excise for the loading and unloading of goods and the embarkation and disembarkation of passengers.

excepted perils. An expression used in contracts of insurance to indicate classes of risk and accident to which cover will not be given.

excise duty. A charge on duty for raising revenue at rates which are the same for both imported and home-produced goods.

excise licence trade. A trade or business for the carrying on of which an excise licence is required.

excise warehouse. A warehouse approved by Customs and Excise for the deposit without payment of duty of goods liable to excise duty.

executive. The body which administers the laws passed by Parliament. It is made up principally of departments of state, which are headed by ministers.

executive director. Generally a full time member of the board of a company, with responsibility for the work of a particular division of its activity.

exempt input tax. Input tax (**q.v.**) which is attributable wholly or partly to a taxable supply (**q.v.**).

exempt supply. A supply of goods or services for the purposes of value added tax which is exempt from any charge to VAT.

expert witness. A witness with specialised knowledge of a particular situation who may give in evidence his/her opinion of technical matters.

export consignment identifier. A number used when goods are exported under the Simplified Clearance Procedure (SCP) for the unique identification of a consignment on pre- and post-shipment declarations.

export control record (ECR). A permanent record showing details of each consignment liable to a Common Agricultural Policy (**q.v.**) charge or eligible for a CAP payment.

Export Credit Guarantee department (ECGD). An organisation designed to help exporters by providing insurance against the risk that buyers abroad might prove insolvent.

export entry. A shipping bill for goods which must be pre-entered before export; in the case of other goods for export, their particulars in prescribed form.

export finance house. A business providing cash to an exporter and credit to an overseas purchaser.

export house. Any person registered for VAT who, in the course of their business in the United Kingdom, arranges or finances the export of goods from the United Kingdom.

export levy. A charge imposed under the Common Agricultural Policy (**q.v.**) on agricultural products exported from the European Community.

export licence. A permit to export a particular article, the sending of which abroad would otherwise be prohibited or restricted.

export refund. A payment under the Common Agricultural Policy (**q.v.**) made to encourage exports from the European Community of certain goods originating there or in free circulation. It bridges the difference between Community prices and those on the world market.

exporter. For customs purposes, includes the shipper of the goods and the person who performs in relation to an aircraft the functions corresponding to a shipper.

ex quay-duties on buyer's account. A contract by which the seller agrees to deliver goods to the buyer at the quay or wharf at a designated port, the buyer to meet import duties and customs charges.

ex quay-duty paid. A contract by which the seller agrees to deliver the goods to the quay or wharf at a designated port, and to meet all import duties and customs charges.

ex ship. A contract by which the seller undertakes to place goods at the buyer's disposal on board a particular ship at the usual unloading point in a designated port.

extradition. A system of reciprocal treaties between countries regulating the handing over of people accused of particular crimes.

extra-statutory concession. Relief granted from tax or duty in certain circumstances by Customs and Excise where not specifically provided for by statute.

ex-works (EXW). A contract under which the vendor packs goods for the buyer at a time and place provided for in the contract within the vendor's premises.

F

factor. An agent who in the ordinary course of his business has authority to buy or sell goods, or raise money on the security of goods. In certain circumstances he can be made accountable for the VAT of his principal.

failure to notify. A civil penalty in VAT law imposed for failing to comply with requirements such as notifying liability for registration or change in the nature of supplies.

false misrepresentation. A false statement deliberately made.

falsification of accounts. The criminal offence of destroying, falsifying or concealing any document or record.

farmer of the Revenue. A person to whom the right of levying duties of Customs and Excise was let for a particular period. The practice finally ceased in 1683.

faro (faro bank). A game in respect of which gaming licence duty is payable for any premises on which it is played.

FAS (free alongside ship). A contract by which the seller undertakes to deliver goods alongside a nominated ship at its loading berth in a specified port.

fast lane. A customs clearance route at the major ports for cargo originating in the European Community.

FC&S (free of capture and seizure). A clause in a policy of marine insurance excluding loss by capture and seizure of the ship and/or the goods.

FCO. A contract under which all transport and insurance costs have been included in the invoice price up to a point specified on the invoice.

feints. The impure part of a distillation, conveyed into a feints receiver.

female servant duty. A tax levied in 1785 on anyone employing a female servant. It increased in proportion to the number employed, but was abolished in 1792.

F H attendance. Attendance (**q.v.**) by a customs officer at places where a charge is only made on Sundays and public holidays.

FIATA. The international organisation composed of national associations of freight forwarders.

fieri facias. A writ obtained for the purpose of seizing a judgment debtor's money and selling his goods.

final consumer. The person at the end of a chain of VAT supplies, who actually pays the VAT charged, and cannot recover credit for input tax. See 'sticking VAT'.

final gravity. The gravity of wash (**q.v.**) when taken to be distilled.

finance agreement. For VAT purposes means an agreement for the sale of goods under which property is not to be to transferred until the whole price has been paid, and under which the seller retains the right to repossess.

Finance Board of the Isle of Man. Certain notifications to the Finance Board in the Isle of Man are equivalent to notification of Customs and Excise.

financial services. The supply of financial services is treated as supplied where received for VAT purposes.

fine. A financial punishment imposed by a court in respect of a crime.

finings. Substances used for the clarification of beer.

firearms. For VAT purposes, means rifles, shotguns, pistols, revolvers and air guns.

firearms certificate. A licence granted by police authority for the district in which the applicant resides, authorising the possession of a firearm and ammunition.

firm. The term applied to a business carried on as a partnership rather than as a limited company.

first and paramount lien. The lien (**q.v.**) which a company may hold over the shares of one of its members who owes it money.

fishes royal. Sturgeon, porpoises, whales and dolphins, which if caught within territorial waters or stranded belong to the Crown.

fishing boat register. A register of all British sea fishing boats operating from a UK port, controlled by the Registrar of Shipping (**q.v.**).

fixed charge. Security for a loan given in respect of certain definite and identifiable assets.

flag discrimination. Special treatment in some matter such as crewing or placing contracts given to the subjects of particular states.

fleet policy. An insurance policy by which several vessels or vehicles belonging to one owner are covered.

floating charge. Security for a loan given over the assets of a person or company in general, and not fixed on certain definite items.

floating policy. A policy of marine insurance describing the contract in general terms, but leaving the name of the ship and other particulars to be inserted later.

flotsam. Cargo jettisoned from a ship which floats upon the surface of the sea.

FOB (free on board). A contract by which the seller must deliver the goods on board a particular ship in a specified port.

FOB airport. A contract by which the seller agrees to deliver goods into the care of a particular air carrier at a specified departure airport.

food. Food of a kind used for human consumption is zero-rated for VAT (Sch. 5, VATA).

Food and Agriculture Organisation (FAO). One of the specialised agencies of the United Nations (**q.v.**), responsible for the development of world agricultural resources.

footwear. Articles designed as footwear for young children and not suitable for older persons are zero-rated for VAT (Sch. 5, VATA).

FOR (free on rail). A contract by which the seller undertakes to load goods onto a specified railway as freight, for a destination nominated by the buyer.

forbearance to sue. A promise not to enforce a legal right.

force majeure. Irresistible force, making the carrying out of a particular act or event impossible.

foreign going ship. A ship trading between a foreign country and the United Kingdom, Channel Islands or the Isle of Man.

foreign port. A port situated outside the United Kingdom, Channel Islands or the Isle of Man.

foreshot. The first running-off of spirit from a distillation.

forfaiting. A system for guaranteeing an exporter immediate payment without liability for default on the part of the buyer overseas.

forfeiture. A consequence of the seizure of goods by Customs and Excise where this liability arises. It involves the loss of title to the forfeited goods.

forgery. The making of a false document in order that it may be used as genuine.

fortification. The mixing in an excise warehouse (**q.v.**) of duty-unpaid made wine (**q.v.**) with duty-unpaid spirits, or of duty-unpaid wine with duty-unpaid spirits (**q.v.**).

forwarder's certificate of shipment. Documentary evidence that shipment has been carried out on a specified vessel.

Forwarders Local Import Control (FLIC). A scheme whereby authorised consignees can obtain clearance of imported goods at their premises rather than at the port of importation.

FOT (free on truck). A contract by which the seller agrees to load goods onto a suitable road transport vehicle for a destination selected by the buyer.

FPA clause. A clause in a policy of marine insurance exempting underwriters from responsibility except for general average, or loss from stranding, burning or sinking.

franchise warehouse. A warehouse approved by Customs and Excise for the warehousing of goods by the warehousekeeper only.

fraud. An untrue statement of fact, made without knowledge of its falsity, or belief in its truth, or without caring whether it is true of false.

fraudulent preference. A transfer of property made to defeat a creditor, amounting to an act of bankruptcy (**q.v.**).

free carrier (FCA). A contract under which the vendor hands goods over to the carrier nominated by the buyer cleared for export at a time and place nominated by the buyer. It has now replaced FOB (**q.v.**) in respect of road transport.

free circulation. Goods imported from outside the European Community on which all import procedures have been completed and all duties, levies or equivalent charges have been paid and not refunded.

free entry. A form of customs entry required to be completed by the importer for goods which are free of duty.

free in and out. In ships' charters, an expression denoting that the shipowner is responsible for all charges except loading, unloading and dry-dock.

free movement of capital. One of the basic aims of the Common Market, which is to get rid of restrictions on the movement of finance between people living in the various member countries.

free of capture and seizure. A clause in a policy of insurance by which the risks of war are excluded.

free of charges. A contract by which the seller of goods includes all delivery charges to a named destination in his price.

free oil. Hydrocarbon oil (**q.v.**) which may be delivered without payment of duty under certain conditions.

free on board value. The amount to be shown by the exporter in customs documentation as the value of the goods being exported.

free pardon. Part of the Royal Prerogative, by which both conviction and sentence are remitted. Customs and Excise enjoys its own powers in this area, which cannot be resisted by a court.

free pratique. Health clearance given to persons arriving in the United Kingdom on a vessel from abroad.

free tenant. A tenant of licensed premises who is under no obligation to obtain his alcoholic drink from a particular source.

free zone. (1) An enclosed area into which goods may be moved without payment of customs duty and similar import charges, including VAT on importation. An extension of the free port (**q.v.**). (2) An area designated within the United Kingdom as a special area for customs purposes.

free zone goods. Goods moved into a free zone (**q.v.**) which while remaining there are not subject to duty, levy or monetary compensatory amount (**q.v.**).

freeboard deck. The deck shown by the deck-line mark on a ship's side.

freeport. An area in which goods may be landed, stored, mixed, blended, repacked, manufactured and reshipped without customs intervention.

freight. A sum of money paid for the carriage of goods by sea under a contract of affreightment (**q.v.**).

freight account. A bill sent by a shipowner to the consignor of goods for the cost of carrying them to their destination.

freight forwarder. Someone acting on behalf of an exporter in the shipping, insurance and documentation of goods.

freight forwarders local import control (FLIC). A form of local import control (**q.v.**) for repetitive traffic specially available to freight forwarders.

freight or carriage paid. A contract by which the seller undertakes to send the goods at his expense to a named destination.

freight pro rata. The entitlement of a shipowner under a contract for the carriage of goods by sea to a proportionate payment where only part of the contract has been fulfilled.

freight release. An instruction from a shipping company to a dock superintendent, instructing him to deliver goods to a particular person.

french roulette. A game in respect of which gaming licence duty is payable for any premises on which it is played.

frustration. The situation where it becomes impossible to carry out a contract.

fuel and power. Fuel and power is zero-rated for VAT (Sch. 5, VATA).

fuel oil. Zero-rated for VAT as fuel and power (Sch. 5, VATA).

full report procedure. A procedure for vessels arriving in the United Kingdom to which certain customs formalities apply.

fully taxable person. Someone who only makes standard or zero-rated supplies, not exempt supplies.

fund raising event. The supply of goods and services by a charity or other qualifying body in connection with certain fund raising events is exempt from VAT (Sch. 6, VATA).

funeral. Certain articles connected with funerals may be entitled to relief from VAT on importation.

future goods. Goods which are to be manufactured or acquired by the seller after the contract has been made.

futures market. A market dealing in crops or commodities not immediately available for delivery.

G

gaming. The provision of any facilities for the playing of games of chance is zero-rated for VAT (Sch. 6, VATA).

gaming contract. A promise to give something to another person on the ascertainment of the result of a game.

gaming licence duty. An excise duty payable by the licensee of premises used for gaming.

gaming machine. For duty purposes, a machine constructed or adapted for playing a game of chance activated by a player inserting a coin or token, where the outcome of the game is determined by the action of the machine.

gaming machine licence duty. A tax payable by the operators of certain categories of gaming machine.

garnishee order. An order forcing a third person who owes money to a judgment debtor to pay it to the judgment creditor instead.

gas oil. Zero-rated for VAT as fuel and power (Sch. 5, VATA).

general agent. A representative who has a general authority to act within certain limits.

General Agreement on Tariffs and Trade (GATT). An international treaty including the majority of world trading nations working together with the general aim of reducing tariff barriers and overcoming trading problems.

General Assembly. One of the principle organs of the United Nations (**q.v.**), in effect the forum for the representatives of all member states.

general average. The sharing of a loss equally between all persons having a pecuniary interest in the preservation of a ship and its cargo, where the loss was the result of a voluntary sacrifice made for the benefit of all parties.

general betting duty. An excise duty on the stake money on off-course bets made with a bookmaker.

general crossing. A crossing on a cheque having two parallel lines, with or without the phrases 'and company', 'not negotiable' or 'account payee only'.

general lien. The lawful retention of goods until all debts due from the owner to the possessor have been paid. An example would be a solicitor's lien over a client's papers until his fees have been paid.

general lighthouse authority. A body which may be entitled to a refund of VAT in certain circumstances under s. 20, VATA.

general meeting. A meeting of a company which includes statutory meetings, annual general meetings and extraordinary meetings (**q.v.**).

general partner. A member of a partnership (**q.v.**) who takes the fullest part in its activities.

general valuation statement (GVS). A system of registration with Customs and Excise which allows an importer to enter goods from a specific supplier without entering a valuation declaration for each importation.

general warehouse. A customs warehouse approved for the warehousing of goods by traders generally.

general warrant. A warrant not naming the person to be arrested, traditionally illegal in the United Kingdom. But see Writ of Assistance.

generalised system of preferences (GSP). A preferential trade arrangement of the European Community in favour of certain developing countries and territories outside the Community.

gentleman's agreement. Sometimes used in situations where the parties do not intend to create a legally binding relationship.

giro. A simplified form of money transfer through banks and post-offices.

Glasgow beer duty. A temporary excise duty of two Scots pence (or one sixth of an English penny) imposed in 1693 on beer sold within the town of Glasgow, to raise money for the building of a quay from the Broomielaw to Duckel's Green.

global assessment. An assessment for more than one prescribed accounting period (**q.v.**).

goatmeat clawback. A charge equivalent to the slaughter premium for goats in force during the week of export.

gold. Certain supplies of gold between Central Banks and members of the London Gold Market are zero-rated for VAT (Sch. 5, VATA).

good faith. Generally used in the sense of honesty, as applied to some action or course of conduct.

goods. For the purposes of Customs and Excise, includes stores (**q.v.**) and baggage.

goods on consignment. Goods sent from one country to an agent in another country, for sale by the agent, who remits net proceeds to his supplier.

goods for testing. Goods for testing are subject to relief from VAT on importation.

goodwill. The advantages accruing to a business from its reputation and connections.

goodwill gifts. Goodwill gifts of a symbolic nature may be entitled to personal relief (**q.v.**) from duty and/or VAT on importation.

government chemist. A public official who takes samples and makes analyses on behalf of government departments.

government legal service. Arm of the Home Civil Service open to barristers and solicitors. Its members are attached to various government departments to provide legal services such as advice and advocacy.

grain cargo. A cargo of which the portion consisting of grain is more than one third of the registered tonnage of the ship.

grantee. In respect of a bill of sale, the person in whose favour a bill of sale (**q.v.**) is granted.

grantor. In respect of a bill of sale, the person assigning an interest in personal property.

grape must. Unfermented grape juice.

gratuitous promise. A promise not enforceable under English law due to lack of consideration (**q.v.**).

gravity. The ratio of the weight of a volume of liquid to the weight of an equal volume of distilled water, where both volumes are measured at 20°C.

Great Britain. The Kingdoms of Scotland and England united in 1707 as the Kingdom of Great Britain.

green channel. The channel to be used by a person entering the United Kingdom who does not exceed the customs allowances, has no goods for commercial use, and no prohibited or restricted goods.

green pound. An expression used within the Common Market for the rate of exchange at which prices agreed for the Common Agricultural Policy (**q.v.**) are converted into pounds.

green rate. The representative rate used in calculating prices under the Common Agricultural Policy (**q.v.**) of the European Community. (See also green pound).

grogging. A process by which spirits are unlawfully taken out of the wood of a cask.

gross domestic product. The total amount of goods and services which a state produces during a particular period.

gross gaming yield. For gaming licence duty, the total value of stakes, minus players' winnings, on games in which the house is banker, and participation charges such as table money.

gross national product. The total amount of goods and services produced in a particular state over a given period, plus or minus the balance on external trade.

gross profit. The total of any profits before expenses are deducted.

group accounts. A statement which must be prepared and laid before a general meeting each year by a company controlling subsidiaries (**q.v.**) other than wholly owned subsidiaries (**q.v.**).

group registration. For VAT purposes, the registration of associated companies under a representative in order to obtain preferential treatment.

group treatment. A system by which associated companies can obtain preferential VAT treatment by using a single registration.

groupage transaction. The aggregation of several small consignments into one transaction.

guarantee. A promise to pay any loss arising from a transaction, where the person making the promise is not connected with the transaction.

71

guarantee approval number (GAN). A number allocated to an exporter to indicate that he has provided the Intervention Board for Agricultural Produce with adequate security to cover potential export charges.

guarantee company. A company the liability of whose members is limited by the amount each has undertaken to contribute in the event of a winding-up.

guarantor. A person undertaking to be responsible for the debt or default of someone else.

H

hand-rolling tobacco. Tobacco sold or advertised by the importer or manufacturer as suitable for making into cigarettes, or tobacco of which more than 25% by weight of the tobacco particles have a width of less than 0.6mm.

harbour authority. Collectively, the officials charged with the maintenance and management of a harbour.

hardship application. An application made in a VAT appeal on the ground that payment or deposit of tax should be excluded, due to hardship.

harmonised system (HS). The harmonised commodity description and coding system.

hazard. A game in respect of which gaming licence duty is payable for any premises on which it is played.

head-licence. the first licence granted by an owner of patent, copyright or similar rights to someone using them. That user may then grant sub-licences.

Headquarters of the Allied Commander in Chief Channel (CINCHAN). An organisation the members of which may be entitled to personal relief (**q.v.**) from duty and/or VAT on importation.

Headquarters of the Commander Allied Maritime Air Force Channel (COMMAIRCHAN). An organisation whose members may be entitled to personal relief (**q.v.**) from duty and VAT on importation.

Headquarters of the Commander in Chief Eastern Atlantic Area (CINCEASLANT). An organisation whose members may be entitled to personal relief (**q.v.**) from duty and VAT on importation.

Headquarters of the Commander Maritime Air Eastern Atlantic Area (COMMAIREASTLANT). An organisation whose members may be entitled to personal relief (**q.v.**) from duty and VAT on importation.

Headquarters of the Supreme Allied Commander Atlantic (SACLANT). An organisation the members of which may be entitled to personal relief (**q.v.**) from duty and/or VAT on importation.

heads of agreement. The main points of a commercial agreement noted as a preliminary step, and to be drawn up more fully at a later date.

health. Articles and substances relating to health are relieved from VAT on importation.

health visitor. The supply of services by a person on the register of health visitors is exempt from VAT (Sch. 6, VATA).

hearing aid. The supply of services by a person on the register of dispensers of hearing aids is exempt from VAT (Sch. 6, VATA).

hearth tax. An assessed tax of two shillings a year imposed in 1662 on every hearth and stove in dwelling houses in England and Wales. It was repealed in 1689.

heat. Zero-rated for VAT as fuel and power (Sch. 5, VATA).

heavy oil. Hydrocarbon oil (**q.v.**) other than light oil (**q.v.**).

hedged bet. A bet which one bookmaker lays off with another bookmaker, which nevertheless is subject to general betting duty (**q.v.**).

helmet. Protective helmets for industrial use and for wear by persons driving or riding a motor cycle are zero-rated for VAT (Sch. 5, VATA).

herbal tea. Zero-rated for VAT as food of a kind used for human consumption (Sch. 5, VATA).

highjacking. The unlawful taking over of control of an aircraft, a criminal act by the laws of the United Kingdom.

high seas. The oceans of the world beyond the jurisdiction of any country's territorial waters.

High Sheriff. The official responsible for putting in the bailiffs by execution of process, and presiding over the Sheriff's Court (**q.v.**).

74

hindrance. To hinder a customs officer in the execution of his duty is a criminal offence.

hire-purchase. An agreement to hire goods for a certain period by paying specified instalments at the end of which the customer has the option to buy them. Certain hire-purchase agreements are exempt from VAT (Sch. 6, VATA).

hiring of goods. The letting or hire of goods other than means of transport is treated as a supply of services where received for VAT purposes.

holder. In connection with negotiable instruments such as cheques and bills of exchange, the person in whose favour it is payable or to whom it has been indorsed, and who holds possession of it.

holder in due course. A person entitled to accept a negotiable instrument free from rights of third parties by accepting it in good faith and without notice of any defect.

holding charge. A criminal charge brought in respect of a lesser offence, while a more serious one is under investigation.

holding company. A company which controls a subsidiary company (**q.v.**) either through its board or by holding more than 50% of its share capital.

holding out. The act of suggesting that a particular situation exists, in order that another person will rely on it.

holiday. The day appointed for purposes of Customs and Excise for the celebration of the Queen's Birthday, together with any bank holiday.

holograms for laser projection. No tax is payable on importation of holograms for laser projection produced by the United Nations or one of its organisations.

home trade ship. A ship engaged in trading between the United Kingdom, and the coast of Europe between the rivers Elbe and Brest.

home use entry. Putting goods onto the market in the United Kingdom.

honorary decorations. In certain circumstances, honorary decorations are entitled to personal relief (**q.v.**) from duty and/or VAT on importation into the United Kingdom.

honour policy. A type of marine insurance with a gambling element, where the assured has no insurable interest. Strictly illegal and certainly unenforceable, but still issued and honoured.

horizontal integration. The linking-up of organisations following the same line of business, so as to cut back on costs.

horses. The subject of a margin scheme (**q.v.**), whereby a dealer is only liable to VAT on the difference between acquisition and disposal prices.

hospice. Certain grants of a major interest by a person constructing a hospice may be zero-rated for VAT (Sch. 5, VATA).

hospital ship. A vessel for carrying the sick, wounded and shipwrecked, exempt from capture in international law.

hot pursuit. In international law, the right of pursuing a ship which has committed an offence in territorial waters (**q.v.**) on to the high seas (**q.v.**).

houseboats. Houseboats for permanent habitation and incapable of self-propulsion are zero-rated for VAT (Sch. 5, VATA).

household effects. Furniture and other articles of ordinary and domestic use, including personal effects (**q.v.**) moved with someone on transfer of residence to this country.

hovercraft. A vehicle designed to be supported when in motion by air expelled from the vehicle to form a cushion of which the boundaries include the ground or water. For VAT purposes, included in the definition of ship.

hoverport. An area on land or elsewhere designed or used for affording facilities for the arrival and departure of hovercraft.

human blood. The supply of human blood, or products for therapeutic purposes derived from human blood is exempt from VAT (Sch. 6, VATA).

human organs or tissue. The supply of human organs or tissue for diagnostic or therapeutic purposes or medical research is exempt from VAT (Sch. 6, VATA).

hungary water. A spirit compounded with flowers of rosemary.

hydrocarbon oil. Materials such as petrol products, coal tar and oils produced from coal, shale, peat, other bituminous substances and all liquid hydrocarbons. Examples are petrol and diesel, and are an important part of central government revenue.

hydrocarbon oil duty. An excise duty on hydrocarbon oil (**q.v.**).

hydrometer. An instrument used to determine the strength and weight of spirits.

I

ice cream. Ice cream does not qualify for zero-rating for VAT (Sch. 5, VATA).

ice lolly. An ice lolly does not qualify for zero-rating for VAT.

illegal contract. An agreement totally without effect in law, e.g. to commit a crime or to break a rule of law. It may nevertheless attract VAT liability.

immature spirits. Spirits which have not been kept in a warehouse for a period of at least three years.

immigration officer. An official employed by the Home Office to control the arrival of aliens at ports and airports in the United Kingdom.

immoveable property. Land and leasehold interests, as opposed to objects and chattels.

imperfect entry. A provisional customs entry which an importer can land and examine goods under surveillance where he has not sufficient information about them to make a full declaration. Also known as a bill of sight.

imperial preference. The former system whereby goods originating in the Commonwealth were admitted duty free or at favourable rates on importation into the United Kingdom.

implied trust. A trust arising where one person buys property, and has it transferred into the name of another person.

import account. The quantity of bulk imports at a port or approved warehouse.

import duty. An *ad valorem* tax imposed on goods imported into the United Kingdom.

importation. The act of bringing into this country from any territory abroad.

importer. In relation to Customs and Excise, includes any owner or other person possessing goods, even temporarily. In relation to goods imported by pipe-line, includes the owner of the pipe-line.

import licence. A permit to import a particular article, the bringing of which into the country would otherwise be prohibited or restricted.

import VAT. VAT on the importation of goods is charged and payable as if it were a duty of customs.

impost. Formerly a term for an additional duty of customs.

inch of candle. Formerly a means of valuing goods imported by the East India Company. They were offered for sale in the City of London, and sold at the highest offer made during the burning of an inch of candle.

inchmaree clause. A clause in a policy of marine insurance making underwriters liable for loss caused by certain prescribed matters in addition to those in the standard form of policy.

inchoate instrument. A negotiable instrument such as a bill of exchange which is incomplete in some way.

inchoate offence. A crime which has not necessarily been carried through to completion, such as a conspiracy or an attempt.

incitement. The encouragement of another person to carry out an illegal activity which in itself is a criminal offence.

income and expenditure account. A statement which every company not trading for profit must put before its members in general meeting every year, giving a true picture of its income and expenditure.

income based apportionment. An apportionment of credit for input tax based on the ratio of income from business activities for VAT purposes, to non-business activities.

income tax. A tax levied directly on income and earnings, and administered by the Inland Revenue. First imposed in 1799.

inconvertible banknotes. Notes without any legal right to demand the exchange for their face value in gold, for example modern banknotes of the United Kingdom.

incorporation. The registration of a company with limited liability.

incorporeal chattels. Rights in or over things such as company shares or copyrights, which are intangible, and can only be enforced by legal action.

incoterms. A set of standardised terms relating to international trade drawn up by the International Chamber of Commerce.

incumbrance. Some liability affecting goods or property, such as a mortgage.

indemnity. A promise to pay any loss arising from a transaction, where the person making the promise is connected with that transaction.

indent. Instructions regarding particulars of goods to be purchased, and the price willing to be paid.

indentures. An agreement drawing up the terms of an apprenticeship between the person apprenticed and his master.

independent contractor. One who can perform a given task as and when he pleases, as opposed to an employee who must work as his employer directs.

Independent Television News Limited. A body which may be entitled to a refund of VAT in certain circumstances under s. 20, VATA.

index vectigalium. A summary of customs duties published in 1670 by the farmers of the Customs (**q.v.**).

indictment. A formal statement of a serious crime prepared for a trial by jury.

indictable offence. A serious criminal offence which can be tried only by a Crown Court.

indorsement. Generally, a signature; particularly, it refers to the acceptance of payment under a bill of exchange (**q.v.**).

indorsement of a writ. A statement on a writ of summons making clear the claim that is being made in a civil case, and the relief sought.

indorser. The person to whom payment is made under a bill of exchange, who signs it on acceptance by the person due to make payment under it.

industrial property. A generic name for property rights such as patents, trade marks and registered designs. Sometimes it is also extended to copyright.

inevitable accident. A collision at sea brought about by an Act of God (**q.v.**).

inferior court of record. A lower court such as a county court which is subject to the supervision of a higher court.

information. The stage prior to the issue of a summons by a magistrate by which a statement or information of the offence complained of is put before a justice of the peace by the individual making the complaint or the prosecutor.

infringement. The act of using without authorisation another person's monopoly right, such as a copyright work or a patented invention. Infringing copies may be subject to a prohibition on importation.

ingrosser. A person who bought commodities in order to sell them at a later date.

inhabited house duty. An assessed tax imposed in 1696, at varying rates. It continued in differing forms until finally abolished in 1924.

injunction. An order restraining a person from doing a particular act.

inland bill. A bill of exchange (**q.v.**) which is both drawn and payable inside the United Kingdom.

inland clearance depot (ICD). A place approved by Customs and Excise, to which goods imported in containers or vehicles may be removed from the place of importation for entry, examination and clearance. Also available for goods intended for export in containers or vehicles so that export controls can be carried out before they are moved to a place of export.

inland navigation. Navigation which is not within the limits of a customs port.

inland rail depot (IRD). Centres for inland clearance, as in inland clearance depots (**q.v.**), but handling only rail traffic, either in train-ferry wagons or containers.

Inland Revenue. The department of state responsible for the administration of direct taxes such as income tax. In certain circumstances information may be exchanged with Customs and Excise.

Inner Temple. One of the four societies entitled to admit people to the rank of barrister by calling them to the Bar.

innocent misrepresentation. A false statement honestly believed in.

Inns of Court. The few societies entitled to admit people to the rank of barrister by calling them to the Bar.

in personam. Of a legal action, in respect of a person. Customs proceedings for condemnation are *in rem*, against the goods, rather than in respect of a person.

input tax. The VAT which has been paid by a taxable person (**q.v.**) on a supply of goods made to him or an importation, in respect of which he is entitled to credit.

in rem. Of a legal action, in respect of an object or thing. An action brought by Customs for the condemnation of goods is *in rem*, rather than *in personam* (**q.v.**).

insolvency. The state of being unable to pay one's debts.

inspector of taxes. Full-time civil servants appointed by the Board of Inland Revenue, responsible for the issue of assessments of income tax.

inspector's bail. The release of a person arrested without warrant on a less serious charge by the officer in charge of a police station where the person arrested will not be brought before a court within 24 hours.

Institute of Legal Executives. An organisation to promote the interests of non-professional employees in solicitors' offices, and operating its own system of examinations for Associate and Fellow of the Institute.

instructions. The case presented by a solicitor to a barrister whom he has retained or instructed to act for his lay client.

insurable interest. The principle that a person seeking protection under a contract of insurance must have a financial interest in the event against which he wishes to provide.

insurance. The undertaking by one person (the insurer) to pay money or confer a benefit on another person (the insured) on the happening of a certain event. Usually applied to contracts of indemnity where an event such as a fire may or may not take place. Certain types of insurance are exempt from VAT (Sch. 6, VATA).

insurance services. The supply of insurance services is treated as supplied where received for VAT purposes.

insured. A person who stands to receive a sum of money or other benefit from another person (the insurer, assurer or underwriter) on the happening of a certain event.

insurer. One who undertakes to pay a sum of money or confer a benefit on another person (the insured) on the happening of a certain event.

intangible assets. Property appearing in the accounts of a business which is incapable of physical ownership. Examples are copyright and goodwill.

intellectual property. A generic expression for property rights such as copyright, registered design, trademarks and patents.

intending trader. A person who has not yet made a taxable supply (**q.v.**), but who registers for VAT on the basis of an intention to make future supplies.

interest. Money paid, generally at a fixed rate, in return for the loan of a sum of money. Interest is now payable on VAT owed to Customs and Excise.

interim dividend. The distribution of profits in hand during the course of a company's financial year where the directors are confident that a dividend will be declared at the end of the year.

interlocutory injunction. A court order which takes effect only until the trial of the main action.

interlocutory matter. An interim or secondary dispute or issue arising during the course of proceedings.

internal drainage board. A body which may be entitled to a refund of VAT in certain circumstances under s. 20, VATA.

International Air Transport Association (IATA). An association of airlines setting tariffs on international routes and seeking to harmonise air transport operations.

International Chamber of Commerce (ICC). A non-governmental organisation representing the world business community at national and international levels.

international coasting voyage. A journey between two countries in the course of which the vessel does not go more than 20 miles from land.

international co-operation information document. A document designed to facilitate international trade by assisting the identification of temporarily exported goods.

International Court of Justice. An organ of the United Nations responsible for settling disputes between member states.

international flight. A flight from a UK airport to an airport situated abroad (or vice-versa).

International Labour Organisation. An organisation of the United Nations dedicated to the improvement of working conditions in every country.

International Monetary Fund (IMF). An international organisation aiming to increase international trade and achieve stability between national currencies.

international petroleum exchange of London. A terminal market (**q.v.**), where supplies in the course of dealing are zero-rated.

international services. The supplies of certain types of international service are zero-rated for VAT.

international voyage. A voyage from a UK port to a port in a foreign country (or vice-versa).

inter partes. Between the parties.

interpleader proceedings. A court hearing to decide conflicting claims over goods seized in execution (**q.v.**) of a court order, or over a debt or goods already the subject of court proceedings.

interport removal. A facility for the removal of uncleared goods from the place of import to another approved port or airport for clearance.

interrogatories. Formal lists of questions delivered by one side to a civil dispute which the other side is obliged to answer.

Intervention Board for Agricultural Produce (IBAP). The body in the United Kingdom responsible for administering the charges and refunds of the Common Agricultural Policy (**q.v.**).

intervention price. An expression used within the Common Market to indicate the price level at which support buying for any commodity can take place for the purposes of the Common Agricultural Policy (**q.v.**).

intervention stocks. Agricultural products under the Common Agricultural Policy (**q.v.**) which have been brought off the market as part of the European Community market support arrangements.

intimate search. A search by a customs officer involving a physical as opposed to a mere visual examination of a person's body orifices.

intoxicating liquor. Alcoholic drink which cannot legally be sold without an excise licence.

internal frontier. A frontier common to two member states of the European Community (**q.v.**).

invert sugar. Cane sugar changed from a non-fermentable to a fermentable form.

investment trust. A company inviting subscriptions for its shares and placing sums received in a wide range of investments.

invisible trade. The export and import of services.

invitee. A person who has accepted an invitation, generally to enter the premises of another person.

invoice. For VAT purposes, includes any document similar to an invoice. Strictly, a tax invoice should comply with requirements specified in regulations.

inward clearing bill. A certificate given to a ship's master acknowledging that all customs requirements have been complied with by a ship arriving from abroad.

Inward Processing Relief (IPR). The relief from customs duty available on the importation of goods from countries outside the European Community for process within the United Kingdom, and eventual export outside the Community.

i.o.u. A simple acknowledgment of debt, which is neither a receipt, a negotiable instrument nor an agreement.

Irish whiskey. Whiskey which has been distilled and matured in Northern Ireland or the Republic of Ireland or partly in one and partly in the other.

islands council. In Scotland, a body which as a local authority may be entitled to a refund of VAT in certain circumstances under s. 20, VATA.

Isle of Man. The Isle of Man and the United Kingdom are treated as a single area for the purpose of VAT.

ISO. A reference to a name approved by the International Standards Organisation.

issued capital. The nominal value of shares which are actually issued in a limited company.

issuing house. An institution such as a merchant bank arranging public issues of new shares and stocks

J

janson clause. A clause in a policy of marine insurance making a stated percentage of loss deductible from all claims for particular average (**q.v.**), the underwriters (**q.v.**) being liable only for the excess.

jetsam. Cargo thrown overboard from a vessel which remains under the surface of the water

jettison. The throwing of goods overboard, in order to save the ship or the remainder of the cargo.

joinder of actions. The linking up of separately commenced court cases on the ground that they are sufficiently close in subject matter and circumstances.

joint and several liability. A situation in which a person having a claim against a number of people can sue them all together, or proceed separately against each.

joint lives policy. A policy of life assurance on the lives of two or more people, which is payable on the death of the first person.

joint stock company. A company trading with a permanent joint stock subscribed by members in the form of transferable shares of fixed amounts.

joint tenancy. Where the share of one of several owners passes on his death to the surviving owners.

journals. Journals are zero-rated for VAT (Sch. 5, VATA).

judge in chambers. A judge not sitting in open court, but for the private hearing of special business, such as bail applications.

judgment creditor. Someone who has obtained a court order for the payment of a sum of money.

judgment debtor. One who owes money as a result of a court's decision against him.

judgment in default. A formal decision in favour of a person who has made a claim where the other side has not defended it.

judgment summons. A court action against a judgment debtor (**q.v.**) in respect of the money owed. Customs and Excise prefer to levy distress (**q.v.**).

judicial notice. The principle that a judge will take for granted matters of such common knowledge that no strict proof of them is needed.

justice of the peace. An unpaid magistrate appointed by the Lord Chancellor, on the recommendation of local advisory committees. Otherwise known as JPs.

juvenile court. A court of magistrates or justices of the peace sitting under special conditions to hear a case against a person under 17.

juvenile court panel. A group of magistrates (justices of the peace) existing in each magistrates court division to deal with cases against persons under 17.

K

keeping house. Applied to the case of an insolvent debtor, who adopts the practice of shutting himself indoors, and not answering to callers.

Kennedy round. The sixth round of multi-lateral trade negotiations of GATT (**q.v.**) which took place between 1963 and 1967.

kerosene. Zero-rated for VAT as fuel and power (Sch. 5, VATA).

know-how. Technical skill, experience on production details which may become the subject of a licensing agreement. Transfers and assignments of know-how may be services supplied where received for VAT purposes.

L

land. The grant of certain interests in or rights over land is exempt from VAT (Sch. 6, VATA).

land charge. Something affecting proprietary rights in land, such as a restrictive covenant or an option to purchase.

land registry. A system of local offices investigating and controlling matters relating to registered land.

landing. Includes, for purposes of customs and excise, alighting on water by aircraft.

landing charges. The initial charges incurred for the off-loading of imported goods.

landlord and tenant. A popular expression for disputes relating to property rights in respect of lettings, concerning particularly the fixing of rent and obtaining of possession.

landside. The area of an airport open to the general public before outgoing passengers pass through customs control.

launching clause. A provision in a policy of insurance specifying the risks accepted during the launching of a vessel.

law assessor. A layman with special expertise in particular fields brought in to assist legal chairmen in certain courts and tribunals hearing cases of a tribunal nature.

law of marque. The provisions of international law governing enemy property seized on the high seas.

law of the flag. The principle of treating a vessel according to the law of the nation under whose flag she sails.

laws of Oleron. An ancient system of laws to control maritime matters which influence a number of European systems, including that of England.

lawyer. The supply of services of a lawyer is treated as supplied where received for VAT purposes.

laytime. The period during which a ship is loading or discharging in harbour.

leaflet. Leaflets are zero-rated for VAT (Sch. 5 VATA).

leasehold. A right to exclusive possession of land, usually for a fixed term of years, and less than absolute ownership.

leasehold enfranchisement. The right of a long-term tenant at a low rent to obtain the freehold or a longer tenancy of the property he occupies.

legacy. Certain legacies are entitled to relief from duty and VAT on importation into the United Kingdom.

legal aid. The official state scheme allowing people below certain income and property levels to obtain assistance with legal costs.

legal estate in land. For practical purposes, either a freehold or leasehold interest.

legal executive. A member of a solicitor's staff who is not himself an admitted solicitor or articled clerk. Formerly known as a managing clerk.

legal mortgage. The tendering of land as security for a loan so that legal interest in that land is established in favour of the lender.

legal mortgage of shares. The transfer of shares to a lender as security for a loan, registering the shares in his name and giving him the legal title.

legal personality. The state of being affected in law by rights and duties. Companies and associates as well as humans are included.

legal tender. Coins or Bank of England notes of current validity.

legal weight. The weight of goods and their immediate wrappings taken together.

legatee. The recipient of a legacy or gift of goods in a will.

legislation. Written rules enacted by Parliament or a subordinate law-making body. Acts of Parliament and subordinate legislation are obviously included, but Customs and Excise also claims the right to legislate by public notice.

legislation clause. A provision in international chartering agreements allowing cancellation if discrimination against foreign shipping is introduced.

legislature. The body responsible for making and amending laws, in the United Kingdom the two Houses of Parliament.

letter before action. A final letter written by a person involved in a legal dispute, threatening action unless his request is complied with.

letter of credit. A procedure by which a buyer of goods in another country makes available in the exporting country, cash which the seller obtains by producing evidence of shipment to a bank.

letter of hypothecation. A document addressed to a bank setting out details of drafts relating to the shipment of goods.

letter of indication. A document of identification used by a traveller holding a letter of credit containing a specimen of his signature.

letter of request. A formal document from the personal representatives of a deceased shareholder to the directors of a company requesting the transfer of shares into their name without referring to their representative capacity.

letter packet. A packet transmitted at the letter rate of postage which contains goods.

levy. Charges under the Common Agricultural Policy (CAP) made at import or export to cover the difference between world and European Community prices.

levy execution. To seize goods in payment of a loan, as in distress (**q.v.**).

levy free import scheme. A scheme to allow inward processing relief on some imports from outside the European Community for use in the production of certain exports.

levying war. An element of the criminal offence of treason widely construed to take in a range of activities which give aid or comfort to the Queen's enemies.

lex domicilii. The law applying in the territory in which a person is domiciled.

liability clause. The clause in a company's memorandum of association which states that the liability of its members is limited and which may not be changed.

licence. The transfer or assignment of a licence is regarded as a service supplied where received for VAT purposes. A licence is a contractual agreement by which a limited use rather than an outright sale is granted.

licence in land. Permission to be on or to make temporary use of land.

licence year. In relation to an excise licence issued annually the period of 12 months ending on the date on which the licence expires in any year.

licensed betting office. Premises which are covered by a betting office licence (**q.v.**).

licensed lighterman. A lighterman authorised by the Commissioners of Customs and Excise to convey bonded goods from one dock to another.

licensed methylator. A person holding an excise licence to methylate or mix spirits or to deal wholesale in methylated spirits.

licensing agreement. A contractual document by which a limited use of the subject matter is granted rather than an outright sale.

lien. The right of one person to possess or control property legally belonging to another. It generally arises in respect of money due (**q.v.** possessory, general, particular, maritime and equitable liens).

lien on shares. The right of a company to sell shares not fully paid up belonging to a shareholder who does not respond to a call on the shares (**q.v.**).

ligan (also ligen or lagan). Property thrown overboard from a ship (jetsam) with a float attached to enable it to be recovered in the future.

light dues. A charge levied on a ship to pay for the maintenance of navigational aids such as lighthouses and buoys.

light oil. Hydrocarbon oil (**q.v.**) of which (a) not less than 90% by volume distils at a temperature not exceeding 210°c, or which (b) gives off an inflammable vapour at a temperature of less than 23°c when tested as petroleum.

limitation of actions. The principle that legal rights which one person has against another shall be extinguished after a certain period of time. Special periods apply in certain areas of customs and excise legislation.

limited company. A company with share capital, the liability of its members being confined to any amount unpaid on the shares they hold.

limited legal tender. A sum of money which can be preferred to discharged debts up to a particular amount only.

limited liability. The principle by which the formation of a limited company protects its members from full personal liability.

limited partner. A member of a partnership who does not assume any management function, but whose liability is limited to his own investment.

limited licence to brew beer. A licence authorising the person to whom it is granted to brew beer not for sale and only for his domestic use or that of his employees in the course of their employment.

linked bingo. The situation where two or more clubs combine to play a joint game of bingo.

liqueur. A spirituous liquor which has been so altered in character by the addition of flavouring matter that it can only be sold commercially under a promotional or characteristic name. An example would be Cointreau.

liquidated damages. A pre-estimate of the damage likely to be sustained if there is any breach of an agreement.

liquidator. An official appointed by the court on the winding-up of a company; if none is appointed, the Official Receiver (**q.v.**) or an administrator will act.

liquidator's cash book. Record of ingoings and outgoings which a liquidator is obliged to maintain in a winding-up of a company.

liquidator's record book. An account of the administration of a winding-up which the liquidator is obliged to maintain.

liquidator's trading account. A record of any business carried on by a company during winding-up proceedings which must be maintained by the liquidator.

litigant in person. A party to a case who can address a court on his own behalf without a barrister or solicitor.

litigation. The process of taking a matter for decision by the courts.

littoral rights. The rights enjoyed by the owners of land bounding on tidal navigable waters.

live animals. If of a kind generally used as food for human consumption, they are zero-rated for VAT.

Liverpool barley futures market. A terminal market (**q.v.**) where supplies in the course of dealing are zero-rated.

Liverpool cotton exchange. The chief market through which passes the cotton destined for the factories of Lancashire.

Liverpool free zone. An area of Liverpool designated as a free zone (**q.v.**) for the purpose of duty and VAT.

Lloyd's list. A daily newspaper of shipping interest published by Lloyd's underwriters.

Lloyd's list law reports. A series of reports of decided cases in matters of specialist commercial interest.

Lloyd's S.G. policy. The standard policy at Lloyds for ships and goods.

load line. A mark on the side of a ship indicating the maximum depth to which it is lawful to load it.

loading broker. A shipbroker acting at a port as representative for shipowners to find and load cargoes for him.

loading time. That period of time within which a vessel or vehicle is to be loaded.

loan capital. Money borrowed by a company through the issue of debentures (**q.v.**), in effect a loan secured by the property of the company.

lob. A mixture of yeast and strong wort added to fermenting wash in order to increase the production of spirit.

local authority. A body entitled to refund of VAT in certain circumstances under s. 20, VATA.

local export control (LEC). The system under which goods for export are taken into customs control at premises.

local import control (LIC). A system of local customs control of imports at the premises of importers who regularly import repetitive traffic as full container loads.

local vat office (LVO). Each taxable person (**q.v.**) is assigned to an LVO, from which his control visits (**q.v.**) are made. They are spread through the United Kingdom on a geographical basis.

lockage. A charge made against a vessel as a kind of toll for passing through a particular lock.

log book. A document kept by the master of a registered British ship in order to record daily events relating to the passage.

Lome Convention. An international agreement linking the states of the Common Market with third world countries having close ties with them. Many are ex-colonies.

London acceptance credit. Credit facilities arranged at a London bank on behalf of a British exporter.

London borough council. A body which as a local authority may be entitled to a refund of VAT in certain circumstances under s. 20, VATA.

London cocoa terminal market. One of the terminal markets (**q.v.**) where supplies in the course of dealings are zero-rated.

London coffee terminal market. One of the terminal markets (**q.v.**) where supplies in the course of dealing are zero-rated.

London diamond market. The principal centre in the world for dealings in diamonds.

London fire and civil defence authority. A body to which in certain circumstances a refund of VAT may be made.

London foreign exchange market. Dealers and brokers operating in the City of London for the exchange of currencies.

London Gazette. The Government's official newspaper for the publication of official news and announcements.

London gold futures market. Formerly a terminal market (**q.v.**). When operating supplies made in the course of dealing were zero-rated.

London gold market. One of the terminal markets (**q.v.**) where supplies in the course of dealing are zero-rated.

London grain futures market. One of the terminal markets (**q.v.**) where supplies made in the course of dealing are zero-rated.

London meat futures market. One of the terminal markets (**q.v.**) where supplies made in the course of dealing are zero-rated.

London metal exchange. One of the terminal markets (**q.v.**) where supplies in the course of dealing are zero-rated.

London money market. The banks, discount houses and merchant banks operating in the City of London to trade in credit and money.

London orphan duty. A special levy on wine and coal shipped into London, for the benefit of orphans of the City of London. First levied in 1694, and abolished in 1889.

London overseas mail office (LOMO). The postal depot through which most air parcels from abroad are sent to receive customs clearance.

London platinum and palladium market. A terminal market (**q.v.**) where supplies made in the course of dealing are zero-rated.

London potato futures market. A terminal market (**q.v.**) where supplies in the course of dealing are zero-rated.

London residuary body. A body to which in certain circumstances a refund of VAT may be made.

London rubber market. One of the terminal markets (**q.v.**) where supplies in the course of dealing are zero-rated.

London silver market. One of the terminal markets (**q.v.**) where supplies made in the course of dealing were zero-rated.

London soya bean meal futures market. One of the terminal markets (**q.v.**) where supplies made in the course of dealing were zero-rated.

London sugar terminal market. One of the terminal markets (**q.v.**) where supplies made in the course of dealing were zero-rated.

London vegetable oil terminal market. One of the terminal markets (**q.v.**) where supplies made in the course of dealing were zero-rated.

London wool terminal market. One of the terminal markets (**q.v.**) where supplies made in the course of dealing were zero-rated.

long dated paper. Applied to bills of exchange with a life of at least three months.

long room. The room where public business is transacted in a Custom House.

loss adjuster. A person who acts for an insurance company to discover the cause of a claim and establish the amount of damage.

lost or not lost. A clause in a policy of marine insurance to cover the situation where a ship may be away from port and the parties to the contract are unaware if it is still in existence.

lottery. (1) A distribution of prizes by lot or chance. (2) The granting of the right to take part in a lottery is exempt from VAT (Sch. 6, VATA).

low value procedure. A simplified export procedure for single consignments below a certain value and weight.

low wines. Weak spirit deriving from the distillation of wash (**q.v.**).

lump sum freight. The full amount agreed between shipowner and charterer for the exclusive hire of a ship for a particular purpose.

Lutine Bell. The bell of the ship 'Lutine' which is formally rung on the floor of Lloyds on the occasion of some grave or important announcement.

M

M1. The total of notes and coins in circulation in the United Kingdom, plus current bank accounts.

M3. The total of notes and coins in circumstances in the United Kingdom plus current bank accounts and deposit accounts.

machine bingo. Bingo played by means of a gaming machine and needing a gaming machine licence from Customs and Excise.

made-wine. Any liquor made from fruit and sugar, and which has undergone a process of fermentation.

magistrate. A judicial officer who adjudicates in less serious criminal cases. There are both unpaid justices of the peace and stipendiary magistrates.

magistrates' clerk. An official generally legally qualified who administers a magistrates' court, and advises lay justices on the law.

magistrates' court. The venue for less serious criminal cases, also known as petty sessions.

major interest. In relation to land for VAT purposes means in England and Wales the fee simple or tenancy for a term exceeding 21 years.

majority verdict. A decision of a jury by no less than ten to two, now acceptable and abolishing the traditional requirement of unanimity.

malice. The intent to commit a criminal act or a civil wrong.

malt. Grain steeped in water, allowed to germinate and dried at a certain stage to stop germination.

malversion. Some form of misconduct by the holder of an official position.

manager. A manager resident in the United Kingdom may in certain circumstances be made accountable for the VAT of a non-resident business.

managing director. Generally a full time member of the board of a company supervising the other directors' activities.

manifest. A document containing full particulars of all items comprising the cargo of a ship or aircraft.

Manx Act. The Value Added Tax and Other Taxes Act 1973 of the Isle of Man.

maps. Maps are zero-rated for VAT (Sch. 5, VATA).

mare clausum. An area of sea closed to general shipping by virtue of the claim of a particular country to exercise jurisdiction over it.

margin scheme. A scheme whereby VAT is in the case of certain second-hand goods only charged on the margin between acquisition and disposal costs.

marine insurance contract. A contract of indemnity by which an underwriter agrees to cover another person (the insured) in respect of any losses to ship or cargo.

marine mortgage. A mortgage registered under merchant shipping legislation by which a boat (but not a share in a boat) is made the security for a loan.

maritime lien. A right over a ship arising in respect of certain specific matters such as salvage or the pay of seamen.

market. A meeting place where vendor and purchaser come together for the purpose of dealing in goods or services.

market overt. Special protection for purchasers of goods of doubtful ownership in certain recognised markets in England and Wales, or any shop in the City of London.

market price. In City parlance the price at which stocks and shares have been bought and sold on the Stock Exchange.

marksman. Someone who cannot write his/her name, but is obliged to sign by making an X.

marriage. Personal relief (**q.v.**) from duty and/or VAT may in certain circumstances be allowed on goods imported by a person changing residence on marriage.

marriage duty. An assessed tax imposed in 1695 on the husband on every marriage where neither was in receipt of alms. It was on a sliding scale according to the social position of those involved, and was abolished in 1706.

marshalling the assets. The order of priority for the payment of a dead person's debts and legacies where his property is not sufficient to meet them all.

master. In relation to a ship, includes any person having or taking charge or command of a ship.

master and servant. An expression describing the situation created by employment.

master's declaration. A declaration by a ship's master giving general information on arrival from a foreign port about the ship, its voyage, and details of the ship's stores.

matches and mechanical lighters duty. An excise duty on matches and mechanical lighters (**q.v.**).

mate. Zero-rated for VAT as food of a kind used for human consumption (Sch. 5, VATA).

mate's receipt. A receipt for goods carried on board, signed by the mate after loading, and later exchanged for the bill of lading.

maturity. The time at which a payable order becomes due for payment.

Mayor's and City of London court. The court for the City of London with county court jurisdiction.

mead. An alcoholic drink made by dissolving honey in water, adding herbs and spices and fermenting with yeast.

mechanical lighter. Any portable contrivance intended to provide a means of ignition. It includes mechanical, chemical and electrical devices.

mechanical lighter duty. An indirect tax imposed on any mechanical or chemical contrivance intended to produce a spark or flame.

medical practitioner. The supply of services by a person on the register of medical practitioners is exempt from VAT (Sch. 6, VATA).

medical treatment. The provision of medical treatment in any hospital or other approved institution is exempt from VAT (Sch. 6, VATA).

medicines. The dispensing by a pharmacist of medicines prescribed by a doctor is zero-rated for VAT (Sch. 5, VATA).

mediterranean pass. A pass formerly issued on behalf of the Admiralty to any ship under a British flag sailing for a destination where capture by Barbary pirates was possible. By agreement with the Barbary states it afforded protection against piracy, but it was discontinued in 1853.

member's club. For bingo duty, any club, miners' welfare institute or similar organisation which is constituted and conducted in good faith as a members' club, has no fewer than 25 members, and is not of a temporary character.

members' voluntary winding up. A voluntary winding up of a company with a statement that a majority of its directors consider it will be able to pay its debts in full.

memorandum of association. A document relating to a company setting out its name, objects and capital, and any limitation on its members' liability.

mens rea. A guilty intention for the purposes of criminal law.

mercantile agent. An agent who in the normal course of his business has authority to buy or sell goods, or to raise money on security of goods.

merchandise marks legislation. Legislation prohibiting misleading descriptions of goods, services, accommodation and other facilities, now replaced by the trade descriptions legislation (**q.v.**).

merchant shipping law. The branch of law which affects the rights and obligations of people operating in commercial navigation at sea.

merger. The combining of two or more undertakings to operate under the name of one of them, or under a new name.

mesne profits. Income from land lost by one person during the time another person wrongfully remains in possession.

messuage. In the law of property, a dwelling-house and any land attached to it.

meter error. The difference between the correct volume and the indicated volume, expressed as a percentage of the true volume.

meter factor. A number obtained by dividing the amount of liquid passed into a prover or through a reference meter by the quantity indicated by the meter under test.

methylated spirits. Spirits mixed in the United Kingdom with some other substance in accordance with regulations made by Customs and Excise.

metropolitan county fire and civil defence authority. A body to which in certain circumstances a refund of VAT may be made.

metropolitan county passenger transport authority. A body to which in certain circumstances a refund of VAT may be made.

metropolitan county police authority. A body to which in certain circumstances a refund of VAT may be made.

metropolitan county residuary body. A body to which in certain circumstances a refund of tax may be made.

midwife. A supply of services by a person on the register of midwives is exempt from VAT (Sch. 6, VATA).

military salvage. The recovery from an enemy in wartime of captured vessels.

minimum import price (MIP). A mechanism of the European Community (**q.v.**) for making sure that particular commodities are declared for customs duty above a minimum value.

ministerial tribunal. A tribunal appointed by a minister or government department to hear appeals from decisions of other tribunals or local authorities.

Ministry of Agriculture, Fisheries and Food (MAFF). The government department responsible inter alia, for policy relating to the Common Agricultural Policy (**q.v.**).

minor. A person under the age of eighteen. Previously known as 'infant'.

minority. The state of being under the age of eighteen.

minutes. The record of a company's general meetings (**q.v.**) and of meetings of its directors and executive, which it is obliged to keep in prescribed form.

misdemeanour. At one time a classification of less serious crimes, now abolished.

misrepresentation. A false statement made to induce a person to enter a contract.

missing trader. Someone who has registered for VAT, but subsequently cannot be traced.

mitigation. Facts put before the court by a person guilty of a criminal offence or his representatives hoping to excuse or diminish the seriousness of the offence.

mitigation appeal. An appeal to the VAT tribunal (**q.v.**) against the amount of penalty assessed in a civil fraud case, where the appellant has sought to co-operate with Customs.

mixed policy. A policy of marine insurance in which a particular period of time and a particular voyage are specified.

moiety. A half, generally in the sense of a half-share in some property.

molestation. To molest a customs officer in the execution of his duty is a criminal offence.

monastery. Certain grants of a major interest by a person constructing a monastery may be zero-rated for VAT (Sch. 5, VATA).

monetary coefficient. A coefficient expressing the extent of depreciation or appreciation of the currency of a member state which is to apply monetary compensatory amounts (**q.v.**).

monetary compensatory amounts. A feature of the Common Agricultural Policy of the Common Market, whereby the accounting for compensation payments is adjusted with currency fluctuations.

money. For VAT purposes, includes currencies other than sterling, though a tax invoice must be expressed in sterling. The issue, transfer, receipt of or dealing with money or order for the payment of money is exempt from VAT.

money bill. A parliamentary measure relating to public finance which must be introduced in the House of Commons, which the Lords cannot amend, and which can become law without their consent. Customs and Excise duties and taxes are introduced in money bills.

moratorium. An agreement to desist from taking action to enforce a debt for a certain period of time.

mortgage. Transaction entered into by the owner of land in which he gives a security over his property in return for the money he borrows.

mortgage debenture. A debenture (**q.v.**) by which some property of the company is pledged as security for the money borrowed.

mortgage of land. Land tendered by its owner as security for a loan of money.

mortgagee. One who lends money to a landowner who has put up his land as security.

mortgagor. A landowner who offers his land or property as security for a loan.

mortmain rule. The former rule that a corporation or company could not acquire land, now abolished.

most favoured nation (most favoured party). A principle of international trading agreement by which a state (or party) can claim the most favourable treatment which has been accorded to any other contracting state (or party).

motor cycle. For VAT purposes, a motor bicycle, motor tricycle or motor scooter (with or without side-car) or a bicycle or tricycle with an attachment for propelling it by mechanical means.

moveable property. Objects and chattels, as opposed to land.

movement certificates. Documentation for the purposes of export and import in Common Market countries, relating to origin and transit security.

multi-fibre arrangement. An arrangement of GATT (**q.v.**) covering the trade in textiles.

multilateralism. Framework for trade between many countries promoted by GATT (**q.v.**).

multi media kit. No tax is payable on the importation of multi media kits produced by the United Nations or one of its agencies.

multinational. A term applied to an organisation whose interests, operations and properties are spread across a number of states.

muniments. Documents giving evidence of a claim or entitlement.

murage. In former times, a toll levied on goods brought into a walled town for sale, and devoted to the upkeep of the walls.

music. Printed, duplicated or manuscript music is zero-rated for VAT (Sch. 5, VATA).

muster roll. A book kept on board a registered British ship containing personal particulars of all persons on board.

N

national transit. A system of moving goods under customs control when import or export formalities are carried out away from the place of importation or exportation.

nationality. Membership of a state or nation governing an individual's political status and allegiance.

natural persons. Human beings, as opposed to companies which the law gives a form of personality.

naturalisation. The grant of the nationality of UK citizenship to a foreigner, at the discretion of the Home Secretary.

nautical assessor. A skilled expert in maritime matters who sits with a judge in admiralty cases to assist on points needing specialised skill.

negative entry. An amount entered in a VAT account (**q.v.**) as a negative amount.

negotiable instrument. A document, all rights in which can be transferred simply by delivery, or delivery with endorsement, such as cheques or bills of exchange.

negotiability. The condition by which a document itself and all rights created under it can be transferred simply by delivery, or delivery with endorsement. Examples are cheques and bills of exchange.

negrohead. A variety of tobacco made up and twisted into rolls resembling the head of a negro.

nemo dat quod non habet. The principle that no one can pass on to another person a better title or right than they themselves enjoy.

net profit. Those profits remaining after the deduction of all expenses.

net running yield. The annual return from an investment expressed as a percentage of its market-price or cost after deduction of income-tax at the standard rate.

neutral spirit. Alcohol so devoid of characteristics that there is nothing to distinguish it from any other type of pure spirit.

new town commission. A body which may attract a refund of VAT in certain circumstances under s. 20, VATA.

newspaper advertisements. Newspaper advertisements are no longer zero-rated for VAT, but are now standard-rated (**q.v.**).

newspaper duty. A stamp duty first levied in 1712 on newspapers, but abolished in 1855.

newspapers. Newspapers are zero-rated for VAT (Sch. 5, VATA).

news services. Supplies of information of a kind published in newspapers is no longer zero-rated for VAT.

next friend. A responsible person appointed to bring an action in court on behalf of some other person, such as a child, not able to deal with it on his/her own account.

night. For customs and excise purposes, the period between 11 pm and 5 am.

no case. A submission which can be made by the defence in criminal cases at the end of the prosecution case. If successful, the case is dismissed without the defendant having to give evidence, or put his case.

nominal capital. The nominal amount of share capital which a limited company is permitted by its memorandum of association (**q.v.**) to issue. Known also as authorised capital.

nominal damages. An award reflecting the view that any loss or damage is purely technical.

nominal value. The face value of a security such as a company share.

nominee company. A company formed generally for the purpose of holding shares in the name of another company, thereby concealing the name of the true owner of the shares.

nominee shareholder. A person officially registered as the owner of shares, where they are in fact really owned by another person.

non annex II goods. Products under the Common Agricultural Policy (**q.v.**) resulting from the processing of basic products. Eligible for refund or levy in respect of the basic products used in their manufacture, although not listed (in annex II) of the Treaty of Rome.

non community country. A state which is not a member of the European Community (**q.v.**). Also known as Third Country (**q.v.**).

non-cumulative preference shares. Preference shares (**q.v.**) which do not carry the entitlement to make good any default in dividend from previous years before ordinary shareholders receive a dividend.

non-exclusive licence. An agreement under which one person acquires the right to use something protected by monopoly rights such as copyright or patents, but cannot prevent a similar right being granted to another person.

non-executive director. A member of the board of a company who is not full-time, but who is intended to contribute specialised expertise which his colleagues may not enjoy.

non-stat. A procedure used for exports of goods in respect of which there is no obligation to collect statistics for the purpose of trade statistics.

non suit. A formal decision by a judge that a person bringing a case has not proved it sufficiently to be allowed to continue.

non-tariff barrier (**NTB**). A barrier to trade which is not by way of tariff, e.g. licensing requirements, national standards and health regulations.

non-voting shares. A category of ordinary share (**q.v.**) in a limited company with restricted voting rights, in order to preserve the influence of the original shareholders.

North West Water Authority. A body to which in certain circumstances a refund of VAT may be made.

normal attendance charge location. An approved place normally attended by customs officers, for which a charge is made only for attendance on Sundays and public holidays.

normal residence. A person's principal place of abode situated in the country where he is normally resident. A person changing his normal residence may in certain circumstances be entitled to personal relief (**q.v.**) from duty and/or tax.

Northumbrian Interim Police Authority. A body to which in certain circumstances a refund of VAT may be made.

Northumbrian Water Authority. A body to which in certain circumstances a refund of VAT may be made.

not guilty. The denial of the charge by a person accused of a criminal offence, by which the prosecution becomes obliged to prove its case; the verdict of a court or jury acquitting an accused person.

not guilty by reason of insanity. A verdict available in criminal cases where the person accused is found not to understand the nature and quality of his acts. It has the status of an acquittal, but the person so found may appeal against it.

not proven. An intermediate verdict available in criminal courts in Scotland, but not in England and Wales. Its effect is that while the person accused has not established his innocence beyond all reasonable doubt there is not enough evidence to find him guilty.

not under command. An expression used to signify a vessel which is not under control.

notary public. An official, often a solicitor, empowered to verify certain types of business documents, and to make particular records.

note of hand. An old-fashioned expression for a promissory note.

notice in lieu of distringas. In share dealings, a notice given by someone having an equitable interest (**q.v.**) in the shares of a company, holding up the transfer of shares registered in the name of another person.

notice of abandonment. In policies of marine insurance, a notice which must be given to underwriters (**q.v.**) on the abandonment of a ship.

noting. A statement appended to a dishonoured bill of exchange noting the fact of dishonour.

notorial act. Something which can only be carried out by a notary public (**q.v.**).

novation. The substitution of a new agreement for one already existing.

nuisance duty. An import duty which costs more to collect than the fiscal revenue raised. The International Chamber of Commerce (ICC q.v.) suggests that they operate at 5% or less.

nuncapative will. An oral declaration in the nature of a will exceptionally regarded by the law as valid in the case of servicemen on active service, and sailors at sea.

nunnery. Certain grants of a major interest by a person constructing a nunnery may be zero-rated for VAT (Sch. 5, VATA).

nurse. The supply of services by a nurse is exempt from VAT (Sch. 6, VATA).

O

oath. A solemn declaration sworn on the basis of an individual's religious beliefs.

obiter dicta. Observations made by a judge in the course of his judgment which is not fundamental to the principle on which he is passing judgment.

objection in point of law. In formally pleading a case, an admission of facts alleged, coupled with an objection that they do not give rise to a case at law.

objects clause. A statement in the memorandum of association of a company of the main purposes for which it exists.

obligor. A person bound under the terms of a bond (**q.v.**) to pay money or carry out some act. Customs and Excise insist on bonds in many areas of activity.

obscene publication. The publication of any material which is obscene, in that it tends to deprave or corrupt, constitutes a criminal offence. There is a prohibition on the importation of obscene or indecent material.

obscuration. The extent to which a hydrometer reading of the strength of spirits is reduced by the presence of sweetening, colouring or other matter.

obstruction. To obstruct a customs officer who is acting in the course of his duty is a criminal offence.

obtaining credit by fraud. A former crime involving the obtaining of a pecuniary advantage by deception, now replaced by the law relating to theft (**q.v.**).

obtaining property by deception. The criminal offence of getting hold of another person's property, with the intention of permanently depriving him of it.

occasional attendance charge location. All unapproved places, and approved places where Customs and Excise attend only occasionally, or as a concession. A charge is levied for all attendances.

occasional licence. A special licence to sell excisable goods such as alcohol and tobacco on special occasions at prescribed places.

occupation. In international law, a method of acquiring territory not already forming part of the dominions of any state.

occupier. In relation to any bonded premises, the person who has given security to the Crown in respect of those premises.

OECD. The Organisation for Economic Co-operation and Development, based in Paris.

off course bookmaker. A person carrying on or intending to carry on bookmaking at a licensed betting office or credit office.

offence triable either way. A criminal offence which can be heard either summarily by magistrates (justices of the peace), or on indictment before a Crown Court.

offeree. The person to whom the offer of a contract is made.

offeror. The person making an offer of a contract.

office of transit. A customs office where goods in transit enter or leave a European Community country.

Official Journal (OJ). The Official Journal of the European Communities. The 'L' series contains legislation, and the 'C' series information and notices.

official receiver. An official who assumes responsibility for the protection of a debtor's property on the making of a receiving order (**q.v.**).

official referee. A circuit judge designated to hear cases involving lengthy consideration of complex documents and accounts.

official seal. A seal fixed by or at the direction of a customs officer, which may be broken or removed only on the direction of an officer.

official secrets. Classified information confidential to the administration of the state, the unauthorised disclosure of which constitutes a criminal offence.

official solicitor. An officer of the Supreme Court of Judicature who acts for people committed to prison for contempt of court, and litigants of unsound mind.

offshore installation. Goods arriving at an offshore gas or oil installation may in certain circumstances be entitled to deferment of duty.

old style committal. A detailed examination by magistrates of the evidence of a serious crime in order to establish whether the matter should be tried by jury. The evidence may be read, as given by live witnesses.

omnibus credit. Credit facilities granted to a shipper of good financial standing allowing drawings against the security of a general lien on the shipper's goods.

on consignment goods. Goods imported for post importation sale in the European Community (**q.v.**) where the value of the sale is not known at the time of importation.

on course bet. A bet made on a racecourse, which is not subject to general betting duty (**q.v.**).

on course bookmaker. A person who intends to carry on or is carrying on bookmaking at a race-meeting.

open account policy. A form of bad-debt insurance by which each invoice not met is written off the total amount insured.

open cheque. An uncrossed cheque which may be paid over the counter to the person holding it, or the person in whose favour it is drawn, or to a person to whom it has been transferred by endorsement.

opening a cheque. The act of nullifying a restrictive crossing on a cheque, so that it can be cashed across the counter of a bank.

open policy. A policy, generally of marine insurance, which does not specify the value of the subject-matter which has been insured.

operative mistake. A mistake of fact as opposed to a mistake of law.

ophthalmic optician. The supply of services by a person on the register of ophthalmic opticians is exempt from VAT (Sch. 6, VATA).

option. The right to bring into force a binding contract at some time in the future.

orderly marketing arrangement (OMA). An ad hoc agreement, usually bilateral, designed to protect domestic industries.

orders. A form of delegated legislation (**q.v.**) made by ministers, usually requiring submission to Parliament prior to coming into force as law.

ordinary resolution. A decision passed at the meeting of a company by a majority of the people present who are entitled to vote.

ordinary shares. The category of shares in a limited company which is entitled to the balance of assets and profit remaining after the payment of preference shares.

organisation for economic co-operation and development (OECD). An international organisation devoted to the expansion of world trade and raising living standards.

organisation registration. The registration for VAT of an organisation, as opposed to the members of that organisation.

original evidence. The testimony of a witness who speaks to facts from his own knowledge.

original gravity. In relation to any liquid in which fermentation has taken place, its gravity before fermentation.

original precedent. A decision of a court which creates and applies a new rule.

originating application. A means of commencing proceedings in the county court.

originating summons. A method of commencing a non-contentious procedure in the Chancery Division of the High Court.

ostensible authority. Powers within the apparent scope of an agent's authority.

outlying provisions. The provisions relating to customs and excise which became law before 1979, and were not re-enacted in the Customs and Excise Act 1979 or the Betting and Gaming Duties Act 1981.

outport. Every customs port in the United Kingdom apart from the Port of London.

output tax. The VAT paid to a taxable person on supplies which he makes, and for which he must account and pay to Customs and Excise.

outs. Formerly applied to casks of wine which had leaked during an inward voyage.

outward processing. The exportation of goods from the United Kingdom for processing abroad and eventual return to this country. It attracts certain relief from duty.

overpaid VAT. Where Customs and Excise have been paid a sum by way of VAT which was not due to them, they are liable to repay it to the taxable person.

overproof. The strength of spirit of which the specific gravity is less than that of proof spirit.

overreaching. A principle of property law which allows obstacles in the way of a purchaser to be overcome, if the obstacle is one of a defined class, and the purchase money is paid to those entitled to receive it.

overriding commission. The commission paid by a company to a main underwriter (**q.v.**) for arranging further contracts to lay off part of his liability with other people.

overriding interest. A right in land not recorded on a land certificate.

overseas countries and territories (OCTs). A category for countries and territories of member states of the European Community (**q.v.**) and thus associated with it.

overseas trade statistics. Information about the export trade of the United Kingdom, published monthly, and serving as economic indicators for government, industry and commerce.

overt act. An act manifesting criminal intent and tending towards the carrying out of a criminal objective.

P

package. A right granted by charter to the City of London in 1641 to examine and pack goods brought there by foreigners for export. The rights were bought out in 1833.

packet boat. A vessel used for the conveyance of passengers by water within the United Kingdom.

packing. All receptacles or packing used in the transport of goods except containers and pallets.

paid-up capital. The total amount which has been paid up on the issued share capital.

paid-up licence. An agreement under which a person taking a licence can make as much use of it as he wishes for one lump sum, as opposed to a royalty agreement.

paid-up policy. A policy of assurance on which no further premiums are due to be paid.

paid-up policy value. The amount to which the sum assured on a life policy would be reduced if a re-arrangement were sought with no further payment.

painting books. Painting books are zero-rated for VAT (Sch. 5, VATA).

pallet. Transport platforms on which goods can be stacked for ready handling.

pamphlets. Pamphlets are zero-rated for VAT (Sch. 5, VATA).

pardon. The right of the Crown to order the amendment of sentence and conviction, reduction of sentence, or substitution of another form of penalty. Customs and Excise enjoy a limited right of pardon.

parish council. A body which, as a local authority, may be entitled to a refund of VAT in certain circumstances under s. 20, VATA.

Parliamentary draftsman. A member of the government legal service (**q.v.**) with special responsibility for drawing up bills and acts of Parliament.

Parliamentary sovereignty. The principle that Parliament can pass any law it chooses, and that there is no law which cannot be altered by Parliament.

parole board. A panel advising the Secretary of State on the early release of prisoners before the conclusion of their sentences.

part performance. A remedy where one person has performed part of a contract normally requiring written evidence but oral evidence exists, and it would be fraudulent of the other person to take advantage of the absence of writing.

participating policy. A policy of life assurance, under which the person assured receives a share of the issuing company's profits.

participating preference shares. Preference shares (**q.v.**) in a category which provides that, after paying a dividend to preference and ordinary shareholders, the participating shares will receive favourable treatment in any further distribution.

particular average. A maritime loss arising from a danger insured against other than a general average loss (**q.v.**).

particular charges. In marine insurance, extra expense incurred for the protection of whatever has been insured.

particular lien. The right of a person in possession of goods to retain them until any debts incurred in connection with those goods have been met. An example would be a tradesman who has carried out repairs on goods.

partition. The right of a joint-tenant to call for the sale of the property, so that each joint-tenant may take his specified share.

partner. A person who has entered into the relations of a partnership (**q.v.**).

partnership. A relationship existing between persons carrying on a business in common with a view to profit.

partnership at will. A partnership without any fixed term, or one which carries on after the time originally set for bringing it to an end.

partnership registration. In VAT law, both a partnership (**q.v.**) and the individual partners may register for VAT purposes.

party and party costs. An amount payable by the unsuccessful party to a civil action allowing all essential charges but not unnecessary ones.

passage. For the purposes of maritime law, a single trip, either outwards or home.

passenger baggage. The clothing and other personal effects of a passenger.

passenger transport authority (or executive). A body which may be entitled to a refund of VAT in certain circumstances under s. 20, VATA.

passing a dividend. The action of a company which decides not to pay a dividend at a time when it would normally be due.

passing-off. A civil action by one manufacturer whose trade has been damaged by another manufacturer using misleading trade descriptions to enhance interest in his own product.

passport. A document giving details of a person's nationality and identity for use when travelling abroad.

patent. An assignment of a patent is treated as a service supplied where it is received for VAT purposes.

patient. A person suffering from a mental disorder who is subject to certain disabilities at law.

patrial. A person who enjoys the right to live in the United Kingdom because of his close association with this country.

patriotic body. A body which in certain circumstances does not have to be registered for VAT solely on the basis of its members' subscriptions.

pavage. In former times, a toll charged on goods brought into a town for sale, and devoted to the upkeep of the roads there.

pawn. A delivery of goods or the documents of title relating to them as security for the payment of a debt or the carrying out of an obligation.

pawnbroker. A person who keeps a shop for the taking of goods as security for money advanced on them.

pawnee. The person to whom goods or the documents of title relating thereto are delivered as security for the payment of a debt or the carrying out of an obligation.

pawnor. The person to whom goods or the documents of title relating thereto are delivered as security for the payment of a debt or the carrying out of an obligation.

paye. The Pay As You Earn system, under which income tax is deducted from wages and salaries by employers, and the balance paid net to employees.

payee. The person to whom payment is directed to be made, in an order such as a cheque or bill of exchange.

payment into court. A device open to the defence in civil claims. If a sum of money is paid into court, and the judge does not award damages of a larger amount, the claimant cannot receive any costs after the date of payment into court.

payment of honour. Where someone such as a banker has refused to pay on a bill of exchange drawn on him, someone else may step in and make payment for the honour of the person whose bill was dishonoured.

payment or deposit. Certain VAT appeals (**q.v.**) shall not be entertained unless the amount which Customs has determined to be payable is paid or deposited with them.

pedlar. An itinerant trader going from door to door offering goods for sale.

penalty liability notice. A notice served by Customs and Excise specifying a penalty period for the purpose of the persistent misdeclaration penalty.

penology. The scientific study of the sentencing of criminals.

peppercorn rent. A rent which is purely nominal.

per. With reference to a statement by a judge 'in the opinion of'.

per curiam. In the view of the court.

peremptory challenge. An objection to a juror without giving a reason for it.

perfect entry. A declaration of goods for customs purposes in final and complete form.

performance. The complete fulfilment of a contract.

performance bond. A sum of money put up as guarantee by a person undertaking a job under contract. Customs and Excise insist on bonds in many cases.

perils. An expression used in insurance contracts to describe those eventualities which are covered, and those which are excluded.

perils of the sea. Applied in contracts of marine insurance to accidents arising in the course of navigation, as opposed to inevitable occurrences.

period entry. A system under which single customs entries for each shipment or removal are replaced by a periodic schedule.

period warehousing. A system under which entries for removal from customs warehousing are replaced by data from a trader's computer, together with periodic schedules.

periodicals. Periodicals are zero-rated for VAT (Sch. 5, VATA).

perjury. The wilful making of a false statement by someone who has taken the oath as a witness in judicial proceedings.

perpetual debentures. Debenture capital (**q.v.**) issued on the basis that the amount lent to the company is repayable only in the event of its winding-up, or some other condition.

per pro (p.p). An indication that the person who actually signs a document is signing on behalf of another person.

per procurationem. A signature 'per pro' or 'p.p.' indicates a limited authority on the part of the signatory, who may not exceed the powers granted by the person on whose behalf he/she signed.

per se. On its own.

perry. A liquor below 8.5% in strength made from the fermentation of pear juice.

persistent misdeclaration. A civil penalty in VAT where there is a material inaccuracy in two prescribed accounting periods (**q.v.**) falling within certain time limits.

persona. A person or thing having personality in the eyes of the law.

personal chattels. Objects such as household goods and clothing, as opposed to objects used for business purposes.

personal effects. Any clothing or goods other than alcohol, reasonably required by a temporary visitor for his private use, not imported for a commercial purpose.

personal luggage. In relation to a person entering the United Kingdom, the luggage he clears from customs control at that time, including any luggage consigned by him as personal luggage which arrives subsequently.

personal property. The section of the law concerned with rights over chattels or physical objects, as opposed to land.

personal relief. Relief from customs duty and/or VAT on importation of property which is available in certain circumstances, and may be either temporary or permanent.

personal representative. In certain circumstances the personal representative of a deceased person may be registered for VAT.

personal service. The act of delivering formal legal documents personally to a party to proceedings generally by a process server such as a bailiff.

personal ties. Family or social ties to which a person devotes most of his time not devoted to occupational ties.

personality. Personal property in the nature of chattels, as opposed to land.

pet food. If canned, packaged or prepared, does not qualify for zero-rating for VAT (Sch. 5, VATA).

petroleum gases. Zero-rated for VAT as fuel and power (Sch. 5, VATA).

petrol substitute. Any liquid intended to take the place of petrol as fuel for internal combustion engines, being neither hydrocarbon oil nor power methylated spirits.

petty assizes. In medieval times, twelve freeholders of a district charged with deciding a dispute over possession of property.

petty sessional division. The area or locality covered by a particular magistrates' court.

petty sessions. Magistrates' courts which hear less serious criminal cases not triable by jury.

pilfering. An expression popularly used to describe the unlawful removal of individual items, as opposed to the removal of an entire package.

pharmaceutical chemist. The supply of services by a person on the register of pharmaceutical chemists is exempt from VAT (Sch. 6, VATA).

philanthropic body. A body which in certain circumstances does not have to be registered for VAT merely because of its members' subscriptions.

philosophical body. A body which in certain circumstances does not have to be registered for VAT merely on the basis of its members' subscriptions.

phoenix company. Applied where a new company rises from the ashes of a company which has gone into liquidation owing money to Customs and Excise.

pilot. A person not forming part of the crew of a ship who is at some stage given control of its movement.

pilotage. Fees levied for acting as a pilot (**q.v.**).

pilotage services. Pilotage services are zero-rated for VAT (Sch. 5, VATA).

pimp tenure. A medieval right to hold land, in return for maintaining women for the king's pleasure.

pipe of wine. A measure of 126 gallons of wine.

piracy. Robbery, violence or murder committed at sea by people not acting under lawful authority of any country.

place of supply. Rules determine whether goods or services are supplied in the United Kingdom, and therefore subject to VAT.

plain British spirits. Spirits in their original state, manufactured in Great Britain or Northern Ireland, and without artifical flavouring.

plaint. File reference for a case in the county court.

plaint note. A document issued by a county court to a person who is commencing a case there.

plaintiff. A person who brings an action in civil law.

plankage. A fee levied on ships in harbour for the use of planks while loading or unloading cargoes at the dockside.

plantation duties. Customs duties originally imposed in 1673 on goods exported from the English colonies in America for destinations other than England.

plea. The response made by a person accused of a criminal offence when asked by a court whether or not he/she admits it.

pleadings. Written statements delivered by both sides to a civil case setting out the arguments each will be putting forward at the trial.

pleasure boat. For personal relief (**q.v.**) any vessel with or without engines for private use, including component parts, normal accessories, equipment, lubricants and fuel.

pleasure craft. A vessel used for private recreational purposes whose crew does not exceed a certain number, subject to customs procedures on arrival in or departure from the United Kingdom.

plea to the jurisdiction. A contention by a person accused of a criminal offence that he has already been found not guilty of the charge.

pledge. The delivery of goods or the documents of title relating thereto as security for the payment of a debt or the carrying out of an obligation.

pledgee. The person to whom goods or the documents of title relating thereto are delivered as security for the payment of money or the carrying out of an obligation.

pledger. The person who delivers goods or the documents of title thereto as security for the payment of money or the carrying out of an obligation.

plimsoll line. A line painted on the side of a ship to indicate the level to which it can safely be loaded.

poinding. In Scotland, a form of diligence (**q.v.**) similar to distress (**q.v.**) and used for the recovery of VAT debts.

poker dice. A game in respect of which gaming licence duty is payable for any premises on which it is played.

police authority. A body which may be entitled to a refund of VAT in certain circumstances under s. 20, VATA.

police court. A term popularly applied to a magistrates' court. Its use is not officially encouraged.

policy. The principal document embodying a contract of insurance or assurance.

political body. Certain political bodies are not registrable for VAT merely on the basis of members' subscriptions.

poll. A procedure for cancelling a vote taken on a show of hands (**q.v.**) at a meeting of a company. It is open to any member present.

pontage. Tolls levied in former times on goods passing over a bridge.

pontoon. A game in respect of which gaming licence duty is payable for any premises on which it is played.

pony. The subject of a margin scheme (**q.v.**), whereby dealers are only liable to VAT on the difference between acquisition and disposal prices.

pool betting duty. A tax charged on all forms of betting by pools, and bets made at fixed odds with a bookmaker.

port. A place appointed as a port by statutory instrument by Customs and Excise.

port authority. The body responsible for the management and maintenance of the area of a port.

port health authority. A body which may be entitled to a refund of VAT in certain circumstances under s. 20, VATA.

port local authority (also joint). A body which may be entitled to a refund of VAT in certain circumstances under s. 20, VATA.

port of adjudication. The port to which a captured vessel is taken in a country with which its owners' country is at war.

port of registry. The port at which a British ship is registered and to which she is regarded as belonging.

port risk policy. In marine insurance, a policy under which cover ends as soon as the vessel leaves its moorings on a new voyage.

port wine. A description which in the United Kingdom may only be applied to wines produced in Portugal.

portage dues. Former rights enjoyed by the Corporation of London to carry all goods between the River Thames, and the premises of foreign merchants in London. Parliament bought them out in 1833.

positive entry. An amount entered into a VAT account (**q.v.**) as a positive amount.

positive rate. A rate of VAT other than zero. When only standard rate exists, that is the positive rate. An extra luxury rate would also be positive, if it existed.

possession. Physical control exercised over a particular article which excludes other people from the same control of the article.

possessory lien. The right of someone in possession of another person's property to keep it or control it until his claims against the owner of the property are satisfied.

post-dated cheque. A cheque bearing a date later than the day of issue, in order to delay payment, and usually to allow payment in of funds to receive it.

post entry. A form of customs entry supplementary to the main entry made to adjust an undercharge of duty.

post horse duty. An assessed tax levied first in 1779 at a rate per mile on any horse let for hire by the mile. It was administered by tollgate-keepers, and abolished in 1869.

post obit bond. A personal security by which a borrower agrees to pay a lender a larger sum than the amount borrowed, to be paid on the death of another person from whom the borrower expects to inherit.

postal packet. Any article sent by post.

postal packet offences. The sending of obscene or prohibited material through the post constitutes a criminal offence.

postal service. The act of sending formal legal documentation by post to the address of a person's solicitor, or if he has none, his last known address.

postal services. The conveyance of postal packets by the Post Office and the supply by it of connected services are exempt from VAT (Sch. 6, VATA).

post shipment declaration. A full export declaration presented after shipment under the simplified clearance procedure (**q.v.**).

postponed accounting system. A system under which a taxable person (**q.v.**) could import goods without immediate payment of VAT, and on his next return accounted for it as input tax and output tax, so that there was no liability to pay unless he was partially exempt. The system was suspended in 1984.

pound breach. A common law criminal offence for breaking a pound to remove cattle which had been distrained on.

pratique. Communication between the crew of a ship arriving from abroad and the inhabitants of a port once it has been established that there was no sickness on the voyage.

precatory trust. A form of trust arising where a person gives property to another person and expresses a wish that it be dealt with in a particular way.

pre-emption clause. A clause in the articles of a private limited company insisting on the offer of any shares for sale being made in the first place to existing members of the company.

pre-entry. A form of pre-shipment declaration (**q.v.**) presented before shipment on a Single Administrative Document (SAD) (**q.v.**).

preference. (1) A system resulting from agreements between European Community and non-Community countries (**q.v.**) as a result of which goods originating in the latter country can be imported at a preferential (which may include a nil) rate of duty. (2) The right to pay any creditor in preference to other creditors of equal standing.

preference shares. Shares of a limited company having preferential status in respect of dividend, and the protection of capital if the company is wound-up.

preferential debt. A debt of a bankrupt enjoying a high priority for payment out from any assets, for example a workman's wages.

preference goods. Goods imported into the European Community from outside at favourable rates of duty on account of the goods originating in one of certain specified countries. A parallel system exists for exports from the Community to such countries.

pre-preferential debts. Debts of a bankrupt enjoying a particularly high priority for payment out from any assets.

preferment of a bill of indictment. The putting forward of an indictment alleging a serious criminal offence against someone.

preferred debt. A debt ranking before certain other categories of debt in insolvency. Certain debts due to Customs and Excise are preferred debts.

prefinancing. A system under which export refund (**q.v.**) can be paid before export takes place, the goods being under customs control either in an approved warehouse or for processing. The goods must be exported within a prescribed period.

premium. An instalment payable under a life assurance policy.

prescribed accounting period. The period prescribed for the accounting and payment of VAT by a taxable person (**q.v.**).

prescriptive right. A right which comes to be recognised in law where it can be shown to have existed openly and without dispute over a long period.

pre-shipment advice. A commercial document submitted for loading purposes under Simplified Clearance Procedure (**q.v.**) or a partly or a partly completed Single Administrative Document (SAD) (**q.v.**).

pre-shipment declaration. A full export declaration on a Single Administrative Document (SAD) (**q.v.**), presented before shipment.

president of VAT tribunals. The person appointed by the Lord Chancellor to be the head of the VAT tribunal system.

Prestwick airport. An area of Prestwick Airport has been designated as a free zone (**q.v.**) for the purpose of duty and VAT.

presumption of advancement. The presumption that an actual purchaser of property intended to benefit the nominal purchaser rather than create a trust in favour of himself.

presumptive charge. Estimated produce of materials employed in the brewing of beer or the distillation of spirits.

pre-trial review. A consideration by the court of matters which will arise in a long trial, in an effort to shorten proceedings and save time and expense.

price-earnings ratio. The market price of a share expressed as the number of years' purchase of current earnings.

prima facie. On the face of things; at first sight.

prima facie **case.** Literally, a case at first sight. It is applied where the side making an allegation demonstrates enough to make the other side contest the issue, and defeats the counter claim that there is no case to answer.

primage and average. Fees customarily paid under a bill of lading (**q.v.**) to the master of a ship.

primary evidence. The best evidence available as a means of proof. An example would be an original document.

prime minister. The leader of the political party commanding a majority in the House of Commons.

primogeniture. The former right of the eldest son to inherit property in the absence of a will. It is no longer applicable in England.

principal. The person on whose behalf an agent acts.

printed matter. For VAT purposes, includes printed stationery but does not include anything produced by typing, duplicating or photocopying. Certain printed matter may be relieved from VAT on importation.

prisage (also butlerage). Wine formerly prised or taken by the King's butler for the King's use from every ship bringing in wine.

prisoner. A defendant or accused person in a criminal case who is remanded in custody. The use of the term is not encouraged at the present time.

prisoner at the bar. The person in the dock who is accused of a criminal offence.

private aircraft. Any aeroplane, airship, balloon, flying machine or glider, with or without engines, for private use, including the component parts, accessories, equipment, lubricants and fuel.

private carrier. A person who carries goods or persons for reward only occasionally or under a special agreement.

private company. A company which may not invite the public to subscribe for its shares, which limits its membership, and restricts the right to transfer its shares.

private effects. Articles intended for the owner's private use not intended for sale or gift to other people.

private international law. The system of law governing disputes between individuals which may involve the laws of more than one country.

private law. Fields of law such as contract, tort and property which control the rights and obligations of individuals between each other.

private nuisance. An unauthorised use by one person of his/her property so as to cause damage to another's property, or to disturb that other person's enjoyment of their property.

private prosecution. A prosecution brought by an individual on his/her own behalf, not through the police or other prosecuting authority.

private tuition. Certain types of private tuition are exempt from VAT (Sch. 6, VATA).

privateer. A privately owned ship which is accrued and engaged by a country at war to attack the vessels or territory of its enemies.

privity of contract. The rule that a person who is not one of those who actually made the contract cannot enforce any right or obligation in that contract.

prize. Something captured at sea from an enemy of the nation, for example one of the enemy's ships.

prize bingo. Bingo where the prizes are other than cash.

prize court. A body set up at the commencement of hostilities to give judgment in cases of ships captured at sea.

prize crew. A group of seamen put on board a ship captured in time of war to sail it into a port of adjudication (**q.v.**).

prize law. The procedures governing the capture of ships at sea in time of war.

probation. An alternative to a prison sentence, under which the person so punished is placed under the supervision of a Probation Officer.

probation officer. A person trained in the supervision of criminal offenders outside the prison system.

process goods. Foreign goods imported for process or repair, and subsequent re-exportation.

process server. A person such as a bailiff whose duties include the formal delivery of legal documents to a party to proceedings.

processing for free circulation (PFC). A scheme under which dutiable goods are imported free of duty, then subjected to a process, after which duty is paid on the processed goods.

procurator-fiscal. A government employed lawyer staffing the state prosecution service in Scotland.

produce broker. A person who arranges for the purchase and sale of raw materials and commodities.

producer gases. Zero-rated for VAT as fuel and power (Sch. 5, VATA).

professional body. The supply to its members by a professional body of services and connected goods referable to its aims and available without payment other than membership subscription is exempt from VAT (Sch. 6, VATA).

profit and loss account. A statement which the directors of a company must put before a general meeting of its members each year.

profit à prendre. A right to take particular material from another person's land.

profits. Those assets of a company not representing capital or earmarked for meeting its liabilities which are available for distribution as dividends.

pro forma. 'For form's sake'. In the case of an invoice, being for purposes of information, rather than an actual charge note.

prohibited goods. Goods subject to a prohibition on importation or exportation, and which are smuggled if the prohibition is broken.

prohibited signal. A signal connected with the smuggling or intended smuggling of goods into or out of the United Kingdom.

prohibition. An order of the High Court to prevent a body from acting unlawfully.

prohibitory injunction. A court order to prevent a wrongful act being carried out or continued.

promissory note. An unconditional written promise to pay either on demand or at some particular time in the future to either a particular person or his/her order, or to the person holding the promissory note.

promotion of trade. Articles for the promotion of trade are subject to relief from VAT on importation.

proof. (1) The strength of alcoholic liquor as ascertained by hydrometer or other approved means. (2) The evidence by which a fact alleged is established.

proof of debts. The procedure under which a creditor may make a claim for compensation from any assets in bankruptcy proceedings.

proof of evidence. A draft made by a solicitor of what it is hoped a witness will say in court.

proof of service. The formal establishment that documents have been properly left with a party to proceedings, either personally or by post.

proper. In relation to the person by, with or whom, or the place at which, anything is to be done; in customs law it means the person or place appointed or authorised for that purpose by the Commissioners of Customs and Excise. Thus 'proper officer'.

proper officer. The person appointed or authorised by the Commissioners (**q.v.**) in respect of any matter in the course of his/her duties.

property. The right of ownership over some item of material or human resources.

property register. One of the Land Registers containing descriptions of registered land by ordnance survey reference and postal address.

proposal form. A term used in insurance for the document on which the person proposing to take out a policy sets out details for the insurance company to consider.

proprietorship register. One of the Land Registers stating the type of title issued, and listing names and addresses of owners.

proprietor. For customs purposes, includes, in relation to any goods, any owner, importer, exporter, shipper or other person for the time being possessed of or beneficially interested in them.

pro rata. In proportion.

prospectus. An invitation to the public by a company to subscribe for shares or debentures.

protected buildings. Certain grants of a major interest by a person substantially reconstructing a protected building may be zero-rated for VAT (Sch. 5, VATA).

protection of minorities. A general principle of company law by which it is sought to maintain a fair equilibrium between majority and minority shareholders.

protection of the revenue. A doctrine applied by Customs and Excise to justify particular courses of action, sometimes sanctioned by statute.

protectionism. The imposition of restrictive or distortive measures to protect a domestic industry from competition from imports or to give its exports an artificial competitive advantage.

protest. A formal statement drawn ıp by a notary public to record the fact that a bill of exchange has been dishonoured.

provable debts. Debts which a creditor is able to prove against the estate of a bankrupt.

provable non-provable debts. Debts which, although strictly capable of being taken into account or proved in bankruptcy proceedings, have been incurred in circumstances where a creditor loses his rights, generally because he/she is on notice.

provisional certificate of registry. A temporary certificate granted by a Registrar of Shipping other than the Registrar of the Port of Registrar, or by a consular officer where a ship has become British while in a foreign port.

provisional collection of taxes. Legislation authorising the collection of taxes at new rates mentioned in a budget resolution, until they are confirmed by Act of Parliament later in the session.

provisional liquidator. An official appointed by the court after presentation of a winding-up petition (**q.v.**) and prior to the making of a final order, in order to protect the assets of the company concerned.

proximate cause. A doctrine of marine insurance that the immediate and not the remote cause of a loss must be taken into account.

proxy. A person appointed by a member of a company to attend a meeting of a company in his place, and to vote on his behalf.

public company. A company limited by shares which is not subject to the restrictions of a private company as to membership, share transfer and invitation to the public.

public examination. A court appearance made by a debtor after the submission of his statement of affairs, or the expiry of the time limit for doing so.

public international law. The system of law governing relations between independent states.

public law. A classification covering constitutional, administrative and criminal law.

public roads. Roads repairable at the public expense.

public stock. Stock forming part of the National Debt, and transferable in the books of the Bank of England.

public trustee. An official who can be appointed as a new or additional trustee by a court, the settlor, or anyone having the power of appointment.

puisne judge. A judge of the High Court (literally, a judge of lower rank).

puisne mortgage. A legal mortgage not having the protection of deposit of title deeds.

punto banco. A game in respect of which gaming licence duty is payable for any premises on which it is played.

pupil. Pupils normally resident abroad may in certain circumstances obtain personal relief (**q.v.**) from duty and/or VAT on importation for scholastic equipment (**q.v.**).

purser. The officer on board a ship whose duty is to look after cargo, crew and passenger documentation.

Q

Q flag. A flag to be flown by a vessel entering United Kingdom territorial waters until such time as all customs formalities have been completed.

qualification shares. The number of shares in a company which its articles may specify must be held by a director of the company.

quantum. The amount, particularly in relation to an award of damages.

quantum meruit. A claim for reasonable payment for work which has actually been carried out.

quarantine. The period during which an animal brought from abroad must be isolated before it can be allowed into the United Kingdom.

quarantine station. The part of a port or airport approved for the importation of foreign animals.

quarter. For VAT purposes means a period of three months ending at the end of March, June, September or December.

quarter sessions. Former criminal court for less serious cases triable by jury. They were replaced by the Crown Court.

quasi. Having the appearance of.

quasi-contract. A principle under which the law implies a promise on the part of one person to pay money to another.

quasi-derelict. Applied to a vessel which has not been abandoned, but where the people left on board are unable to navigate in safety.

Queen's Bench Division. The section of the High Court dealing chiefly with civil disputes such as contract, negligence and defamation.

Queen's Bench Master. An official appointed from barristers of at least 10 years standing who decides disputes arising during a civil case. His decisions can be taken on appeal to a judge.

Queen's warehouse (King's warehouse). A Crown Customs warehouse named according to the gender of the reigning monarch, for the storage of goods seized or detained by Customs and Excise.

question of law. A matter on which the judge should rule in a criminal trial, as opposed to questions of fact. There is wider scope for appeals on questions of law.

quick report procedure. A procedure available to certain vessels arriving in the United Kingdom, to which certain customs formalities do not apply.

quit rent. Formerly, a payment in order to rid oneself of certain feudal obligations or services.

quorum. The minimum number who must be present before a meeting, particularly of the board of a company, can begin.

quota. Quantative restrictions, sometimes imposed on individual supplier countries. Once filled, either no additional imports are admitted or if admitted, only at a higher tariff rate. A quota restricts the amount of goods which may benefit from a preference.

quoted company. A public limited company, the shares in which have been given a quotation on a recognised stock exchange.

R

racehorse duty. An assessed annual tax first imposed in 1784 on every horse starting in a race that year. Collected by Clerks of the course, it was abolished in 1874.

rack rent. The highest sum which can be obtained as rental for a property of a particular value.

rackee of Turkey. An aromatic liqueur compounded in Turkey and neighbouring lands from spirits and certain spices.

racking. The process of drawing off wines and spirits from one cask or vessel into another.

racking warehouse. A distiller's warehouse (**q.v.**) approved for the temporary storage only of spirits produced at the distillery.

RAF airfield. Goods arriving at an RAF airfield may in certain circumstances be entitled to deferment of duty.

railway passenger duty. A stamp duty first imposed in 1832 upon train passengers other than holders of cheap tickets. It was abolished in 1929.

rates. Local taxes on occupiers of property in the area of a local authority to raise revenue for it.

ratification. The act of confirming that something is legally binding.

ratio decidendi. The fundamental principle underlying a judgment or decision given by a judge.

raw spirits. Spirits which have not been rectified or compounded.

real property. The section of the law concerning itself with rights over land.

realty. Rights over land.

reasonable excuse. A limited form of mitigation which may apply in certain VAT civil penalties.

rebated heavy oils. Oil such as gas oil or kerosene on which the rate of duty has been reduced from that applicable to DERV (**q.v.**).

receipt. A written acknowledgment that a certain sum of money has been received.

receipt account. An account of the quantity of bulk imports raised by a warehousekeeper at a warehouse approved by Customs and Excise.

receiver. In certain circumstances a receiver may be separately registered for VAT.

receiver for the metropolitan police district. A refund of VAT may in certain circumstances be paid to the receiver under s. 20, VATA.

receiver of wreck. The Collector of Customs and Excise (**q.v.**) for a particular locality who acts on behalf of the Department of Trade in cases of wreck or salvage.

receiving order. An order making the Official Receiver (**q.v.**) the guardian of a debtor's property, and halting all legal action against the debtor.

reciprocity. (1) The principle that trade negotiations should be mutually advantageous to all parties through the reciprocal exchange of concessions on a multilateral basis. (2) The theory, inconsistent with GATT principles, that each country should be entitled to reciprocal trade advantages with each of its trading partners on a bilateral basis.

recognizance. A bond (**q.v.**) or personal security given by a person to ensure the attendance of himself or another person at a court hearing.

reconstruction. The transfer of its assets by one company to a new company, which adopts a new capital structure and the shareholders of the first company. The first company is wound up in the process.

record office. The location in which official records are kept for reference, in particular records of decided cases.

recorder. A part-time judicial appointment given to barristers and solicitors, generally to test their suitability for appointment as circuit judge.

Recorder of London. The chief judge of the Central Criminal Court (Old Bailey).

records. All persons registered for VAT are obliged to keep such records as Customs and Excise may require.

rectification. The principle that where a document wrongly expresses the intention of the people concerned, the court will allow it to be altered.

rectified spirits. Pure spirits of the third extraction which have not been flavoured.

rectifier. A person holding an excise licence to rectify spirits.

red channel. The Customs channel for persons entering the United Kingdom who exceed the customs allowances, have goods to sell, or have prohibited or restricted goods.

reddendum. A clause in a lease specifying the amount of rent reserved to the lessor.

redeemable debentures. Debenture capital (**q.v.**) the nominal amount of which the company is obliged to pay at a certain date, or in a prescribed way.

redeemable preference shares. A category of preference shares (**q.v.**) which may be bought back by a company if certain specified conditions are met.

reducing. The process of reducing the strength of spirits by the addition of water.

reduction of capital. The diminishing by a company of its share capital, a practice strictly forbidden without the authority of the Court.

re-examination. Questions put by an advocate to one of his/her own witnesses to re-establish his/her case after cross-examination by the other side.

re-exportation. The exportation of goods which have previously been imported into the country, as opposed to the exportation of goods which originated in the United Kingdom.

refer to drawer. A comment made on a cheque by the bank on which it is drawn when dishonouring it.

refinery. Premises approved by Customs and Excise for the treatment of hydrocarbon oils, or for the production of energy for use in the treatment of hydrocarbon oil.

regional council. In Scotland, a body which as a local authority may be entitled to a refund of VAT in certain circumstances under s. 20, VATA.

register of business names. Formerly, a register kept of firms, companies and partnerships trading under any style other than the name or names of the owner, or the corporate name of a company.

register of charges. A record which a company is obliged to keep of all liabilities secured on its assets, such as mortgages and charges. A general register is kept by the Registrar of Companies, and an individual one by each company.

register of directors and secretaries. A record which every company is obliged to keep giving personal particulars of each director and its secretary.

register of directors' interests. A record which a company is obliged to maintain of shareholdings of its directors and other relevant interests which they acquire.

register of members. A record of the members of a company which must be maintained, and its whereabouts notified to the Registrar of Companies.

register of substantial individual interests. A register which a limited company is obliged to maintain of the particulars of anyone acquiring £10 or more in nominal value of its relevant share capital (**q.v.**).

registered club. A club occupying premises at which alcohol is sold, which must be registered with the justices of the peace for the area.

registered company. A corporation formed under the Companies Acts.

registered debentures. Debenture capital (**q.v.**) payable to a registered holder and transferable in the same way as share capital.

registered excise dealer and shipper (REDS). A revenue trader authorised to import and pay excise duty on goods from another European Community member state without having to submit customs entries for clearance of the goods.

registered office. The official location of a company, the address of which must be lodged with the Registrar of Companies.

registered person. A person making taxable supplies (**q.v.**) who has registered for VAT.

registered security. Stocks or shares the title to which is evidenced by the issue of a certificate.

registered tonnage. Gross tonnage or cubic capacity of a ship expressed in tons of 100 cubic feet each, less approved deductions.

registrable. In relation to VAT, means liable or entitled to be registered for VAT.

registrar. The senior administrative officer of the VAT tribunals.

registrar of companies. A public official whose duty is to record the incorporation of companies.

registrar of criminal appeals. An official in charge of administrative matters in the Court of Appeal (Criminal Division), who organises the documentation and hearings.

registrar of shipping. The chief officer of Customs and Excise in a port designated as a registry port (**q.v.**). He/she acts for the Department of Trade in matters relating to the registration of British ships.

registration limit. The financial limit of turnover which determines a person's liability to register for VAT.

registration number. The number allocated by the Commissioners to a taxable person in the certificate of registration for VAT issued to him.

registration period. In respect of a taxable person (**q.v.**) in VAT, the period commencing on his effective date of registration and ending on the day before the beginning of his first tax year (**q.v.**).

registry port. A United Kingdom port at one of which a British ship (**q.v.**) has to be registered.

regulation. A form of Common Market legislation binding as law within member countries without further legislation in that country.

regulations. A form of delegated legislation (**q.v.**) made by ministers usually requiring submission to Parliament prior to coming into force as law.

regulatory amount. A charge applied to certain tariff sub headings in the wine sector for Spanish products.

reimportation. The importation of goods which have previously been exported from the United Kingdom.

re-insurance. The insuring by an underwriter of the whole or part of a risk he has himself insured, in order to relieve himself of the burden of it.

relation back. The process by which the title of a trustee in bankruptcy over a bankrupt's property is backdated to a time three months prior to the debtor being adjudged bankrupt.

release. An abandonment of his outstanding rights by someone who has carried out his side of a contractual bargain.

release on licence. A scheme for the early release of prisoners before the conclusion of their sentence on the advice of the Parole Board.

relevant month. In relation to a person liable to register for VAT, the month at the end of which he becomes liable to be registered.

relevant share capital. Issued share capital of a class carrying the entitlement for the shareholder to vote at all general meetings.

relief. Freedom from liability to pay duty and tax, if certain rules or conditions can be fulfilled.

religious body. Certain religious bodies are not liable to register for VAT merely on the basis of member's subscriptions.

remand. An adjournment of a criminal case to a later date, the defendant being either remanded in custody or on bail.

remission. The waiving of import or export duties which have not yet been paid, to be distinguished from repayment (**q.v.**).

rendering sparkling. A process applied to wine or made-wine by raising it to certain levels above atmospheric pressure in particular kinds of container.

rent action. An action brought by a landlord against a tenant for arrears of rent.

rent charge. A sum of money payable annually in respect of landed property.

renunciation. The refusal by one person to carry out his/her side of a bargain, thus leading to a breach of contract.

repair and maintenance concession. A system under which clearance facilities may be made available at certain aerodromes to assist commanders of aircraft arriving for major repair and maintenance.

repayment. The total or partial refund of import or export duties which have been paid, as distinct from remission (**q.v.**).

repayment supplement. An additional amount payable to a taxable person by Customs and Excise where in certain circumstances Customs delay a credit for input tax or repayment of VAT.

repayment trader. A person registered for VAT whose credit for input tax exceeds his/her liability for output tax on a regular basis, so that he/she is usually in the position of receiving money from Customs and Excise.

repeatability. A measure of agreement between meter errors obtained for a succession of proving runs under identical operating conditions.

reply. A written statement by the person making a claim in a civil case in response to a defence.

reporting restrictions. Restrictions on reporting by the media of certain court proceedings, particularly committals, which may be waived by the accused person.

Reports of Tax Cases. A series of published decisions in cases relating to specialised revenue matters.

representations. Statements made to induce a person to enter a contract.

representative action. Court proceedings taken by one person on behalf of another person or persons as well as himself.

representative member. The company chosen for registration purposes in a VAT group (**q.v.**).

representative rate. The rate of exchange used to convert agricultural prices expressed in European Currency Units (**q.v.**) into national currencies. Also known as the Green Rate (**q.v.**).

reputed ownership. Applied to goods deemed to be under the control of a bankrupt with the consent of the owner, and therefore owned by the bankrupt.

request. The document filed to start a case in the county court.

requisitioned meeting. A meeting of a company called at the behest of the holders of not less than £10 of its paid-up voting capital.

requisition on title. Inquiries on behalf of a prospective purchaser of a house to the representatives of the seller on matters on the title deeds of the property.

resale loss policy. A form of bad-debt insurance, covering part of any loss where a supplier has taken back goods from an insolvent debtor.

rescission. The setting aside of a contract, or part of it.

rescue of distress. A common law indictable offence for removing goods which have been distrained on. A civil penalty now applies in VAT.

reserve. That part of the profits of a limited company which have been held back from distribution to the shareholders by way of dividend.

reserve capital. Any section of the uncalled capital (**q.v.**) of a limited company which has been stated by special resolution to be incapable of being called-up, unless in a winding-up of the company.

reserve fund. That part of the profits of a limited company which have been held back from distribution to the shareholders, and invested in easily realisable assets.

res judicata. The principle that a matter can no longer be questioned once a court has given its decision on it.

resolution. A decision taken at a meeting of a company, which may be either special, ordinary or extraordinary (**q.v.**).

resolution requiring special notice. A special decision relating to the appointment and removal of company directors and auditors to which prescribed provisions for notice and advertisement apply.

respondent. In general, the other side in a case taken on appeal by an appellant; in particular, the person against whom a VAT appeal is made — i.e. Customs and Excise.

respondentia bond. A form of security pledging the cargo of a ship for the repayment of money borrowed for the purposes of a voyage.

restitution order. A court order directing the return of property to a particular person.

restraint of princes. A limitation of liability inserted in contracts to guard against property being detained by official authority in foreign countries, against the owner's wishes.

restraint of trade. The restriction of competition between businesses or of a person's freedom to follow his trade or profession.

restricted goods. Goods subject to a restriction on importation or exportation.

resulting trust. A trust arising where a beneficiary predeceased someone who had set up a trust in their will, and the property is consequently held for the benefit of the personal representatives of the dead person.

retail scheme. One of several special schemes for accounting for VAT which may be operated by a business in the retail trade.

retailer's invoice. A VAT invoice which a retailer is obliged to supply in certain limited circumstances.

return day. The last day specified for the lodging of a particular document.

returned goods relief. A scheme whereby goods exported from the United Kingdom or the European Community may be imported with total or partial relief from duty or tax.

revenue. The income of the state. In popular speech applied to matters relating to its collection and administration, e.g. 'the protection of the Revenue'.

revenue reserve. That part of any reserve (**q.v.**) held back by a limited company, which may not be distributed to the members in due course.

revenue trade. Any activity or facility for the carrying on of which an excise licence is required.

revenue trader. A person carrying on a trade or business subject to any of the revenue trade provisions of Customs and Excise legislation.

reverse charge. In respect of supplies of services received from abroad, a system whereby the recipient of services is treated as though he had supplied the services himself in the United Kingdom.

reversion. The right of occupation which returns to the owner of freehold on the expiry of a lease.

reversioner. A person who enjoys an interest in land which will continue after a person with a loss or interest such as a tenant has ceased to occupy it.

revocation. The withdrawal of an offer in contract.

right of abode. For immigration purposes, the right of a person to live in the United Kingdom.

right of angary. The right of any country in time of war to take over property on its territory, subject to compensation.

right of approach. In international law, the right of a warship to approach a vessel in order to verify its nationality.

right of audience. The right to speak or conduct a case in court enjoyed exclusively by a barrister in the higher courts, and by a barrister or solicitor in the lower courts. Officers of Customs and Excise enjoy certain rights of audience.

right of convoy. The right claimed in time of war by some states to search neutral ships in convoy under the protection of their own navy. The United States is an advocate of the doctrine.

right of establishment. The right to set up an economic activity in any country, generally free of controls not also imposed on domestic industry.

right of support. The right of a landowner not to have the support of his building or land affected by activities on adjoining land.

right of visit. In international law, the right of a belligerent ship in time of war to stop a neutral merchant ship, and check whether it is assisting the enemy in some way.

ring. A combination of business interests to regulate the supplies of a class of goods so as to raise its price.

riparian owner. The owner of land on one bank of a river or stream, whose rights extend half-way across the river-bed.

riparian rights. The rights enjoyed by the owner of land adjoining non-tidal waters.

river purification board. A body which may be entitled to a refund of VAT in certain circumstances under s. 20, VATA.

road fuel gas. Any substance gaseous at a temperature of 15°C and under a pressure of 1013.25 millibars, and which is for use as fuel in road vehicles.

road vehicle. Any vehicle licensed for use on public roads, whether or not so used, or actually used on public roads, whether or not so licensed.

rollback. The gradual phasing-out of existing protective measures which are inconsistent with GATT principles.

romalpa clause. A provision inserted in commercial contracts attempting to keep ownership in goods until particular conditions have been fulfilled, in particular, that full payment has been made.

rosa solis. A spirit compounded with the juice of the sundew or rosa solis plant.

round charter. An agreement by which a ship is chartered for an entire round trip.

royal assent. The formality by which the sovereign consents to a bill which has passed through both Houses of Parliament becoming an act, and thus passing into the law of the land.

rub-down search. A physical examination by a customs officer which is neither an intimate search (**q.v.**) nor a strip search (**q.v.**).

rule of law. The principle that all citizens of this country are subject to the same laws, and that no one can be punished for something not expressed to be illegal.

rules. A form of delegated legislation (**q.v.**) made by ministers, usually requiring submission to Parliament prior to coming into force as law. An example is the VAT Tribunal Rules.

rules of navigation. The internationally accepted principles which control the movement of ships navigating near enough to each other for a collision to be possible.

rummage. The searching of a ship by Customs officers to ensure that no prohibited or dutiable goods are on board.

S

sailaway boat. A boat exported under its own power, and zero-rated for VAT under an extra-statutory concession (**q.v.**).

salvage. The reward payable by the owners of a ship or its cargo to any persons saving it from wreck, capture or loss, who are under no obligation to act.

salvage agreement. A contract by which the person in charge of a ship in distress accepts the services of people offering to rescue it.

salvage lien. The right which a salvaging vessel enjoys over anything which it has rescued at sea.

salvage services. Salvage services are zero-rated for VAT (Sch. 5, VATA).

samples. Samples may be taken by Customs and Excise of any goods of which a person is making supplies for VAT, for the protection of the revenue.

sans frais. An indication that a person signing a commercial document such as a bill of exchange does not wish to accept liability for expenses.

sans recours. An indication that the person signing accepts no responsibility.

savings account. The operation of a savings account is exempt from VAT (Sch. 6, VATA).

scale discharge. The terms under which bulk cargo from a ship is discharged as laid down in the chartering agreement.

scavage. Dues formerly paid by foreign merchants to the Corporation of London on goods brought into the City for sale. It was abolished in 1833.

scheduled territories. The countries comprising the Sterling Area for the purposes of exchange control (**q.v.**), now abolished. Payment of sterling outside these territories could only be done with Treasury consent.

scheme of arrangement. (1) A settlement between a debtor and his creditors entered into after the start of bankruptcy proceedings. (2) A procedure for altering the rights of a class of shareholders in a company.

scholastic equipment. For the purposes of personal relief, means household effects representing the normal furnishings for the room of a pupil or student, clothing, uniforms, and articles normally used by pupils or students for studies, including calculators and typewriters.

school. The provision of education or research by a school is exempt from VAT (Sch. 6, VATA).

scotch whisky. Whisky which has been distilled and matured in Scotland.

sea coals. Coals carried coastwise to the Port of London from Newcastle and neighbouring ports.

seaman's articles. A seaman's formal documentation containing his contract of service.

seaman's lien. The rights which a merchant seaman enjoys over ship and cargo as security for his unpaid wages.

seaman's will. A will made by a seaman at sea in respect of which strict requirements as to age and written formality are relaxed.

search warrant. An authorisation granted by a justice of the peace on sworn information permitting the entry and search of named premises. See also writ of assistance.

secondary evidence. Non-original or substituted material put forward as a means of proof.

secondary legislation. Legislation in statutory instruments and orders which has not been debated by the full Houses of Parliament.

secondary residence. Any place of abode, other than a normal residence (**q.v.**), where a person resides. Household effects imported for a secondary residence may in certain circumstances be entitled to personal relief (**q.v.**) from duty and/or VAT.

secondary resident. A person who, without being normally resident in the United Kingdom or the Isle of Man, has a home there which he/she owns or is renting for at least 12 months.

second-hand aircraft. The subject of a margin scheme (**q.v.**) and therefore dealers are only liable to VAT on the difference between acquisition and disposal prices.

second-hand boats. The subject of a margin scheme (**q.v.**), and therefore dealers are only liable to VAT on the difference between acquisition and disposal prices.

second-hand caravans. The subject of a margin scheme (**q.v.**), and therefore dealers are only liable to VAT on the difference between acquisition and disposal prices.

second-hand cars. A category of goods where dealers are entitled to operate a second-hand scheme (**q.v.**), and are eligible to be taxed only on the margin.

second-hand electronic organs. The subject of a margin scheme (**q.v.**), and therefore dealers are only liable to VAT on the difference between acquisition and disposal prices.

second-hand firearms. The subject of a margin scheme (**q.v.**), and therefore dealers are only liable to VAT on the difference between acquisition and disposal prices.

second-hand motor cycles. The subject of a margin scheme (**q.v.**), and therefore dealers are only liable to VAT on the difference between acquisition and disposal prices.

second-hand scheme. Schemes for giving relief from VAT on the importation or supply of certain second-hand goods. Such schemes protect dealers against distortion of tax.

second mortgage. A further tendering of property as security for a loan by a landowner who has already taken out a mortgage on that property.

secure transport. Road vehicles, rail wagons or tank craft sufficiently secure for the transport of goods on which excise duty has not been paid.

secured creditor. (1) In bankruptcy, a person having a charge or lien (**q.v.**) over any property belonging to the bankrupt. (2) A creditor in a more favourable position at the winding-up of a company, whose debt is secured against specific assets which must be realised in his favour.

security. Customs and Excise may require a person to provide security as a condition of making supplies or receiving input tax (**q.v.**).

security for costs. An order that one side to a civil action be made to give some guarantee that costs incurred can be paid.

secured debenture. Debenture capital (**q.v.**) issued in respect of a loan where some or all of a company's assets have been mortgaged as security.

seeds. Seeds and certain other items of propagation are zero-rated for VAT (Sch. 5, VATA).

seizure. The act of taking possession of a thing by lawful authority of the state. Goods liable to forfeiture in Customs and Excise law may be seized.

select committee on statutory instruments. A committee of the House of Commons which deals with the delegated legislation (**q.v.**) passing through the House. It scrutinises Customs and Excise subordinate legislation.

selectivity. The imposition of safeguard restrictions on a single supplier nation, rather than non-discriminatory against all suppliers.

self-billing. The practice in VAT of customers receiving approval to make out tax invoices on behalf of their suppliers.

self-executing. Used to describe laws made outside the United Kingdom which take effect in this country without having to pass through Parliament.

self-governing colony. A colonial territory having a responsible government of its own.

self-supply. The use in the course of a business of goods acquired or produced in the course of that business. Generally treated for VAT purposes as a supply to and by that business, thus eliminating any tax distortion.

sentence. The penalty imposed by a court following a plea of guilty or finding of guilt in a criminal case.

separation of powers. The theory that there are three branches of government, legislative, executive and judicial, which must never duplicate each other. This may be infringed when Customs and Excise purport to legislate by public notice.

septic tank. Emptying a septic tank is zero-rated for VAT as a sewerage service (Sch. 5, VATA).

sequestration. A writ against a person disobeying a court order allowing a number of people to take possession of his property until he complies with the order.

serious misdeclaration. A civil penalty in VAT where a return misstates a person's VAT liability, or an assessment understates a person's liability, and that person does nothing to correct it.

service. The means by which official court documents are brought to the attention of a particular individual, e.g. by personal delivery.

service occupancy. A requirement that an employee should live on certain premises in order to carry out his/her tasks more effectively.

services. In VAT law, anything which is not a supply of goods, but which is done for a consideration.

servient tenement. Land subject to a profit a prendre or an easement such as a right of way.

set-off. A cross-claim made by the defendant that a particular sum owed by the defendant to the claimant should be taken into account.

settled land. Land subject to any kind of settlement which restricts the succession to it.

settlement. The period on the Stock Exchange within which settlement for transactions must be made, or carried into the next settlement.

settlor. One who creates a trust by deed or will.

several fishery. A private fishing right dating from time immemorial, or granted by statute.

severalty. Something held by a single person, rather than a shared ownership.

severing the indictment. An order to split charges brought on one indictment into separate trials, on the basis that they are not sufficiently connected.

sewerage services. Certain types of sewerage service are zero-rated for VAT (Sch. 5, VATA).

share. The interest of a shareholder or member of a limited company, as measured by an amount of money.

share capital. The nominal value of shares actually issued in a limited company.

share certificate. A certificate issued under the common seal of a limited company establishing the ownership of the registered holder to the shares referred to.

share-hawking. The practice, now forbidden by criminal law, of fraudulently attempting by direct approach to persuade people to buy shares in worthless companies.

share premium account. The account which a company is obliged to maintain if it issues shares at a premium (**q.v.**), in which amounts equivalent to any premiums must be lodged.

share-pushing. The action, forbidden by criminal law, of fraudulently attempting to induce people to invest in worthless companies by advertisement or circular.

share warrant. A document which may be issued by a public company stating the entitlement of the bearer to the shares referred to, and any dividends. As a negotiable instrument, it is transferable by delivery.

shares. The issue, transfer, or dealing with any shares is exempt from VAT (Sch. 6, VATA).

shares at a discount. The issue of company shares on the condition that the entire liability of the shareholder is less than the full nominal value of the shares. This practice is illegal without the authority of the court.

shares at a premium. Company shares issued at a price above the nominal value of those shares, which does not need the consent of the court.

shebeen. Premises in which unlicensed alcoholic drinks are sold.

sheepmeat clawback. A charge equivalent to the slaughter premium in force in respect of sheep during the week of export.

Sheldon statement. The doctrine that where Customs and Excise with full details of the facts have given a VAT ruling or misled someone to their detriment, an assessment based on the correct position will only be raised from the date the error was brought to the attention of the person concerned.

sheriff. An ancient office which formerly involved great powers in such matters as tax collection. Now much reduced in function.

sheriff court. A Scottish court having limited jurisdiction in both civil and criminal matters.

sheriff's court. A court conducted by the High-Sheriff or under-Sheriff to assess damages where a person has allowed judgment in default to be signed, or to assess the worth of the land of a person unsuccessful in a court action.

ship. Ships over 15 tons gross tonnage not designed or adapted for recreation or pleasure are zero-rated for VAT (Sch. 5, VATA). For VAT purposes, ship includes hovercraft (**q.v.**).

shipmaster's lien. The rights which the captain of a ship enjoys against the cargo as security for payment of the seamen's wages.

shipment. The loading of goods onto a ship, hovercraft or aircraft prior to export.

shipowner's lien. A lien (**q.v.**) which a shipowner has over goods which he has carried on a sea passage, against the payment due to him.

shipped bill of lading. A bill of lading (**q.v.**) which is made out only once the goods to be carried have been stowed on board the vessel.

shipper. The person who consigns or delivers goods to a vessel for transportation to a particular destination, for a particular charge.

shipping agent. A person who represents a shipping company in a particular location or territory.

shipping bill. A document in prescribed form which the exporters of dutiable or restricted goods must produce for examination prior to shipment.

shipping note. Documentation accompanying goods delivered to the place of shipment for export.

shipping value. In insurance matters, the cost of the goods paid by the person insuring them, plus shipping and insurance costs.

ship's articles. The document which contains the agreement between the captain of a ship and its crew.

ship's marks. Details of name, port of registry, tonnage and draught which must be marked on a ship prior to registration.

ship's master. The person appointed by the owner of a registered British ship to navigate it.

ship's report. A document in prescribed form which the master of a ship must lodge in duplicate at the port of arrival, giving details of crew and cargo.

ship's slops. The clothing supply store for seamen on board ship, which may not be liable to VAT on foreign voyages.

ship's stores. Dutiable goods permitted to be shipped duty free by crews of vessels leaving a UK port for an overseas destination.

shipwork relief. Relief from customs duty in respect of goods imported for the construction, repair, maintenance, conversion, filling out or equipping of certain categories of ships and vessels.

short committal. A formal hearing before magistrates at which written statements and documentary evidence of a serious crime is handed in prior to trial by jury.

short term policy. A policy of life assurance payable only if death takes place within a specified period.

sight draft. A bill of exchange endorsed 'cash against documents' CAD (**q.v.**).

sighting. The act of presenting a bill of lading to a ship's master so that release of the goods may be obtained.

simple contract. A contract where no special form is needed, only the presence of consideration (**q.v.**).

simplified clearance procedure (SCP). A system under which exporters of goods not requiring special control can put in an abbreviated customs pre-entry or approved commercial document at the time of export. Full statistical information is provided after export.

simplified period entry scheme (SPES). A procedure allowing importers or their agents to submit monthly computerised summaries of imports of free circulation Community goods for statistical and VAT purposes.

simplified procedure for import clearance (SPIC). A system applying to the import clearance of goods of a value not exceeding a particular value.

simplified procedure value (SPV). A scheme for the speedy clearance of fresh fruit and vegetables.

single administrative document (SAD). A single document which has replaced the numerous import, export and transit forms previously used for customs declaration.

single bond. A personal security for the payment of money or the carrying out of some other act which has no condition attached to it. Bonds are frequently required by Customs and Excise.

single premium policy. A policy of life assurance by which only one premium is paid, at the time it is taken out.

sinking fund. A sum of money set aside for the eventual repayment of a debt.

sister ship clause. A clause in a policy of marine insurance making the underwriters (**q.v.**) liable to the owner of a ship colliding with another ship owned by the same person.

SITPRO. An independent executive UK body sponsored by the Department of Trade and Industry with the aim of simplifying international trade procedures.

skimming. The removal of damaged goods from a particular container, so that only undamaged goods are left.

slander of goods. A form of injurious falsehood (**q.v.**) giving rise to a civil action for wilfully disparaging the merits of another trader's products.

slander of title. A form of injurious falsehood (**q.v.**), giving rise to a civil action for wilfully casting doubt on another person's entitlement to property.

sleeping partner. A member of a partnership who assumes no responsibility for the running of a business.

slip ('The Slip'). A document prepared by an insurance broker noting the terms of a proposed policy of marine insurance, and initialled by underwriters to the extent of any risk they are prepared to accept.

slip rule. A VAT tribunal chairman (**q.v.**) has the power to correct an error in a document containing his decision or direction.

small beer. A weak table beer, originally sold at a duty inclusive price of six shillings per barrel or less.

small claims' court. Either the registrar's court, which hears claims under a certain limit, or special courts which may arbitrate in such cases with the agreement of the parties.

small scale bingo. Bingo either (1) promoted by members' clubs, miners' welfare institutes and similar organisations or (2) played at travelling fairs or amusement arcades under licence.

small ship. For customs purposes, a ship not exceeding 100 tons register, or a hovercraft of any size.

smuggling. The criminal offence of importing or exporting goods without paying the duty or in contravention of a prohibition.

social law. Particularly where betting and gaming duties are concerned, an expression used by Customs personnel about non-Customs and Excise legal provisions.

software protection. The doctrine that computer software, such as programs, can be subject to legal protection from copying via the copyright or patent systems. (Intellectual property may be subject to protection from imported copies which infringe.)

sold note. A contract note sent by a seller to a buyer setting out terms and conditions of an oral contract.

sole licence. Usually relating to patents, where the owner of the patent licenses the use to a single person, but himself retains the right to use it.

sole proprietor. A person working on his own account as a business, and not as a company or in partnership.

solicitor. A member of one of the two branches of the legal profession. He or she has direct contact with the public, and generally undertakes a wider range of work than a barrister.

solicitor-general. One of the two Law Officers of the Crown, and a political appointment. Deputises for the Attorney-General in the capacity as adviser to certain government departments and prosecutor for the Crown.

solicitor-general for Scotland. The junior of the two law-officers of the Crown in Scotland; it is a political appointment.

solus agreement. A commercial contract by which one person agrees to buy all supplies from the other person.

sound recording. The music, song or other sounds fixed onto a gramophone record or tape; in the United Kingdom it may be subject to copyright protection.

South Sea Company. Incorporated in 1711 by charter enjoying the sole British trade round southern America from the Orinoco on the East, to the most northerly Spanish possessions on the West. Its rights were abolished in 1816.

Southampton free zone. An area of Southampton has been designated as a free zone (**q.v.**) for the purpose of duty and VAT.

sovereignty of parliament. The doctrine of the supremacy of Parliament, according to which Parliament can pass any law it pleases. Now curtailed by membership of the European Community (**q.v.**).

special agent. A representative taken on by his principal for a particular purpose only, or for a single commission.

special and differential treatment. A principle of the General Agreement on Tariffs and Trade (GATT q.v.) recognising tariff and non-tariff preferential treatment for developing countries.

special crossing. Its effect is that a cheque can be paid only to the bank nominated, or to another bank acting as its agent.

special damages. The sum of money actually needed to compensate an injured person for a particular loss.

special drawing rights. An arrangement between member states of the International Monetary Fund to settle debts between themselves by drafts on a special fund.

special examiner. Someone appointed by a court to take the evidence of a witness (usually a witness unable to attend court in person).

special indorsement. An indorsement on a negotiable instrument such as a bill of exchange indicating to whom payment is to be made.

special local control. A taxable person (**q.v.**) with a poor compliance record may be placed under special control of his local VAT office.

special resolution. A decision passed by not less than three-quarters of the members present and voting at a company's general meeting (**q.v.**), where not less than 21 days' notice of intention to propose the matter as a special resolution has been given.

specialty contract. A contract made by deed requiring signature and sealing.

specie. Money in coin, as opposed to paper money.

specific bequest. The gift in a will of something which can be definitely identified.

specific goods. Goods which have been identified and agreed upon at the time that a contract is made.

specific duty. A duty based on the unit quantity of the goods on which it is imposed.

specific performance. An order that a person who is in breach of an obligation should be forced to carry it out.

spent conviction. A previous conviction at some time in the past, which should not be taken into account in relation to the person concerned, particularly when being sentenced for a new offence.

spent lees. The residue of the distillation of low wines in a pot-still distillery.

spent wash. The remains of the distillation of wash in a distillery.

spillage. Applied to both solid and liquid goods which have accidentally come out of their containers.

spirit maturation warehouse. A warehouse approved by Customs and Excise for the storage of spirits in cask for maturation.

spirits. Any fermented liquor containing more than 40° of proof spirit.

spirits of wine. Rectified spirits of the strength of not less than 43° above proof.

spirits safe. A secure box with transparent panels designed to enclose the tail or outlet pipe of the worm (**q.v.**) or condenser.

spoilt beer. Beer which has become unfit for use before retail sale, and which on return to the brewery is eligible for remission of duty.

sports competition. The grant of a right to enter certain sports competitions is exempt for VAT (Sch. 6, VATA).

spot market. A market dealing in existing stocks for immediate delivery.

spot price. A price for cash payments, as opposed to payment at some future time.

staff. The supply of staff is treated as a service supplied where received for VAT purposes.

stag. A speculator buying a new issue of shares hoping its price will rise because of over-subscription, so that he can sell at a profit.

stake money. The total amount paid or due to be paid by the person making a bet with the bookmaker.

stale bill of lading. A bill of lading (**q.v.**) which has been presented late to a consignee.

stand by for the crown. The form of words by which the prosecution makes known an objection to a juror, the right to do which has now been reduced.

standard exchange relief (SER). A system of giving relief on replacement goods imported in exchange for goods exported or to be exported from the United Kingdom for repair outside the European Community (**q.v.**).

standard export levy. The charge payable when certain agricultural goods are exported to non-EC countries.

standard of care. The degree of care which it is necessary for the defence to have reached in order to meet successfully an action for negligence.

standard rate. The normal rate at which VAT is charged on goods and services which are not exempt or zero-rated.

standard shipping note. A standardised document for the delivery of conventional cargo into a port receiving area in the United Kingdom.

standing committee. A parliamentary committee which gives clause by clause examination of every bill referred to it.

standing order. A written authority from a customer to a bank, instructing it to pay a certain sum, to a nominated person on a stated date.

standing time. The period which must elapse between an account of spirits being declared in an entry book, and their removal from the vessel in which the account was taken.

Stannaries. Tin-mining areas of Devon and Cornwall, the miners in which enjoy special privileges.

starting. Emptying wine or spirits into a cask or vat.

statement in lieu of prospectus. A statement to be filed by a company which has not issued a prospectus to the effect that all directors have accounted for any liability on their shares.

statement of affairs. Documentary information to be sworn on oath to be presented to the Official Receiver (**q.v.**) prior to the first meeting of creditors.

statement of capital. A document to be filed at the time of incorporating a company, stating capital for assessment of any duty.

statement of claim. A written statement setting out the facts on which a claimant in a civil action is going to rely.

statistical information. Information collected by Customs and Excise in connection with VAT which may in certain circumstances be disclosed.

static slip. In measuring hydrocarbon oil, the passage of oil without registering, when manipulated at very low flow rates.

Statistical Office of the European Communities (SOEC). An organisation of the European Community charged with the collection and dissemination of statistical information.

statute. A written law which has passed through first, second and third readings in both Houses of Parliament, and has received the Royal Assent (q.v. Act of Parliament).

statute-barred. A legal right or debt which can no longer be enforced, because the time for bringing a law suit has run out.

statutory corporation. An undertaking such as the British Gas Corporation formed under a special Act of Parliament.

statutory declaration. In company law, a statement filed on behalf of a company with the Registrar of Companies to the effect that certain preliminary conditions have been complied with.

statutory instrument. Any measure enacting delegated legislation (**q.v.**) by order, rule, regulation, bye-law or order in council.

statutory meeting. A general meeting of the members of a public limited company, which must take place within three months of it commencing business.

161

statutory report. A document which must be given to the members of a company prior to the statutory meeting (**q.v.**) following commencement of business. It gives particulars of the administrative and commercial position of the company.

statutory tenant. A tenant who enjoys the protection of the Rent Acts against eviction and unilateral increases in rent.

statutory trust. The division of property left in a will equally between beneficiaries in a particular class.

statutory water undertaker. A body which may be entitled to a refund of VAT in certain circumstances under s. 20, VATA.

stay. A putting into suspension of an order made by a court. Customs and Excise enjoy powers to stay proceedings.

stay of proceedings. The bringing to a halt, either temporary or permanent, of a case being heard by a court.

sterling area. The Scheduled Territories (**q.v.**) for the purposes of exchange control (**q.v.**). Payments could only be made outside them with the consent of the Treasury. Exchange control has been abolished.

sticking VAT. VAT which is actually paid by the ultimate consumer of goods or services, without any opportunity to recover credit for input tax.

still. Any equipment for distilling or making spirits.

stipendiary magistrate. A solicitor or barrister of at least seven years' standing appointed to adjudicate in less serious criminal cases.

stock exchange ('The House'). A market for the purchase and sale of stocks and shares.

stockbroker. A member of the Stock Exchange acting on behalf of members of the public as agent for the sale and purchase of stock.

stocks. The issue, transfer, receipt of or dealing with any stocks is exempt from VAT (Sch. 6, VATA).

stop for freight. An application to the person having control of goods to hold them up until a carrier has been paid money owed for transporting them.

stop notice. An order to a banker to stop payment on a cheque drawn by the account holder giving notice. In share transactions, a notice by someone having an equitable interest in shares to stop the transfer of shares registered in the name of another person.

stoppage *in transitu*. The right of an unpaid seller of goods who has parted with possession of them to stop and repossess them before they have reached the purchaser.

store floor. An area approved at a Customs and Excise airport (**q.v.**) for the deposit in bonded warehouse of dutiable goods intended as aircraft stores (**q.v.**).

stores. Goods for use in a ship or aircraft including fuel and spare parts and other articles of equipment, whether or not for immediate fitting.

straight bill of lading. A bill of lading (**q.v.**) which cannot be negotiated, but under which goods must be delivered to a particular person named.

strandage. A toll formerly charged for depositing goods on a beach.

stranding. The running of a ship onto a sea-shore, which may be either accidental or voluntary.

street price. The price at which stocks and shares have been bought and sold, outside the Stock Exchange, generally after close of business. Also applied to the black market valuation of prohibited drugs.

strength. The alcoholic strength of any liquor, the ratio of volume of alcohol to volume of liquor being for Customs and Excise purposes expressed as a percentage.

stress of weather. Bad weather conditions which may affect the carrying out of the terms of a contract.

strict liability offence. A criminal offence which can be committed without the guilty person having formed any criminal intent. Also known as a strict liability offence. Numerous examples are to be found in Customs and Excise legislation.

strict settlement of land. A means of keeping landed estates within a family primarily by creating successive life interests in favour of eldest sons.

strike clause. A provision made in contracts by which it is sought to limit the effect of loss, damage or delay caused by industrial action.

strip search. A physical search by a Customs Officer which may involve the removal of clothing worn next to the skin.

strong waters. An expression applied to all imported spirits other than brandy.

student. A student resident abroad may in certain circumstances obtain personal relief (**q.v.**) from duty and/or VAT on importation of scholastic equipment (**q.v.**).

sub-charter. A contract made by a person chartering a ship to sub-let all or part of it to other people.

subject to contract. A phrase indicating that the parties do not intend to be bound until a formal contract between them has been executed.

subject to equities. The taking of a benefit subject to rights which may be enjoyed by third parties.

sub judice. Under judicial consideration. It is a serious contempt of court to enter into public discussion in the media of a matter in any case before the courts, which is said to be *sub judice*.

submission of no case. A submission by the defence, usually at the close of the prosecution case, that the prosecution has not shown a strong enough case to allow the matter to continue to be tried.

subordinate legislation. Orders, regulations and rules having the force of an Act of Parliament, but made by somebody outside Parliament to whom the power to make them has been deputed by Parliament.

subpoena ad testificandum. A summons to compel a witness to attend court to give evidence in person.

subpoena duces tecum. A summons to compel a person having control of a particular document to produce it for a court hearing.

subrogation. The substitution of one person for another as a creditor, and where the debtor has died, the right to stand in his/her executor's place. In insurance, the principle that an insurer who has paid out on a loss is entitled to the benefit of every right which the insured would have.

subscribed capital. That section of the shareholding of a limited company which has been paid for in cash.

subsidiary. A company under the control of another company either through its board or by holding more than 50% of its shares.

subsidies code. An appendix to the General Agreement on Tariffs and Trade which gives examples of export subsidies that it regards as undesirable.

subsidy. Government support for domestic producers aiding their competitiveness in domestic or export markets.

substantial damages. An award to compensate for the actual financial loss sustained by the injured person.

substituted service. The bringing of a court document to the notice of an individual by special steps, where normal service has proved impossible.

substitutional legacy. A gift by will in substitution for another gift, where it is clearly not intended that the two should be in addition to each other.

sub-underwriting. An agreement by which a main underwriter (**q.v.**) contracts with other people to assume a proportion of his own potential liability.

succession. The transfer of a person's property on his death either by will, if he has made one, or according to legal rules if he has not.

Suez Canal clause. A clause in a policy of marine insurance providing that grounding of a ship in the Suez Canal is not regarded as stranding for the purposes of exclusion of liability.

sugar levy. A charge on the added sugar content of certain processed fruit and vegetables.

sui juris. The condition of being of full age and able to meet one's legal responsibilities.

sum insured. The total amount which an insurance company is liable to pay under a policy of insurance.

summary judgment. A means of avoiding full trial in a civil action under which the plaintiff claims that there is no defence to the action.

summary jurisdiction. Trial without jury exercised by a magistrates' court. Many Customs and Excise offences are triable in this way.

summary offence. A less serious criminal offence which can be heard only summarily before a magistrates' or justices' court.

summary trial. A trial before magistrates (justices of the peace).

summing-up. The review of the evidence and law given by the judge to the jury at the end of a criminal trial.

summons. An order issued by a justice of the peace to a person being accused of a criminal offence to appear before him/her on a particular day to answer the charge.

summons for directions. Procedure whereby directions are given by the court as to the manner in which the trial of the main issue is to be conducted.

superior courts of record. A classification embracing the Supreme Court of Judicature, the House of Lords and the Judicial Committee of the Privy Council.

supervening impossibility. A situation where a contract is to be regarded as at an end because of some fundamental change of circumstances.

supplemental petition. A formal statement in divorce proceedings which may be used to bring up matters taking place after the case started.

supplementary assessment. A further assessment of VAT which can be raised by Customs and Excise in certain circumstances where the correct amount of VAT was not assessed initially.

supplementary trade mechanism (STM). A licensing system for certain products from Spain and Portugal, and some non-European Community Countries, replacing ordinary Common Agricultural Policy procedures.

supply. (1) A parliamentary expression relating to the provision of finance to the Crown to fund the organs of the State. (2) A supply of goods or services attracts VAT unless it is an exempt supply. All forms of supply are included, but not anything done other than for a consideration.

supply services. Annual charges on state expenditure for such items as the armed forces and revenue collection departments.

support. A right which every piece of land is entitled to expect from land which adjoins it.

Supreme Court of Judicature. This is made up of the Court of Appeal, the High Court and the Crown Court.

Supreme Headquarters Allied Powers Europe (SHAPE). An organisation whose members may be entitled to personal relief (**q.v.**) from duty and/or VAT on importation.

surcharge liability notice (SLN). A notice served on a person registered for VAT specifying a period within which he becomes liable to the default surcharge (**q.v.**).

suppression. The collection of VAT by a taxable person which he/she does not account for to Customs and Excise.

surety. A person who undertakes to be answerable for the debt on default of someone else; also the sum offered as guarantee.

suretyship. An undertaking or guarantee to answer for the debt or default of another person.

surgical treatment. The provision of surgical treatment in any hospital or approved institution is exempt from VAT (Sch. 6, VATA).

surplus stores. The unused remainder of goods which were permitted to be shipped duty-free for consumption by crews of ships sailing to foreign destinations from United Kingdom ports. Duty becomes payable on their return to the United Kingdom.

surrender value. The amount which insurers are prepared to pay at any time in discharge of a life insurance policy.

survivorship. The principle that on the death of one of a number of joint owners of property, that property vests in the surviving owners.

suspended sentence. A punishment imposed by a court in respect of a crime whereby the offender does not go to prison unless he commits another crime within a certain period of time.

suspense account. An account into which sums of money are paid on an interim basis, if for some reason they cannot immediately be paid into the account of ultimate destination.

suspension. A variety of import duty relief, under which duty is never paid, so long as the goods or products made from them are exported.

sweets. Any liquor made from fruit and sugar which has undergone a process of fermentation.

syndicate. An association of business interests to regulate markets and prices.

T

table A. A model set of articles of association annexed to company legislation, which a public limited company may adopt in whole or in part.

table beer. Beer sold in the 19th century at a price not exceeding 1d. per quart.

tacking. The process whereby an earlier mortgagee may gain priority in repayment over any further loans.

tafia. A rum distilled in the French West Indies from the refuse of sugar cane.

tailings (feints). The impure portion of the distillate from a low-wines still or patent still.

take-over. The merging of two companies by means of one company buying a controlling interest in the other.

take-over bid. An offer circularised to members of a company offering to purchase their shares so as to give the person or company making the offer a controlling interest.

take-over panel. A watchdog body representing a number of financial institutions to ensure that procedures relating to company take-overs are not abused.

taking steps. Taking steps with a view to the fraudulent evasion of VAT is a criminal offence.

takings at sea. The stopping on the high seas of neutral merchant ships, so that they may be taken into port for examination of cargo.

talking books for the blind. Talking books for the blind and severely handicapped are zero-rated for VAT (Sch. 5, VATA).

TARIC. The integrated tariff of the European Community (**q.v.**). An acronym for *Tarif Integré des Communantes Europeenes*.

tariff. A tax or duty imposed on imports.

tariff (The Tariff). A statement of all duties of Customs and Excise prevailing in the United Kingdom, now extended to cover the European Community.

tariff escalation. The application of higher duties as the degree of processing of a product increases.

tariff peaks. Levels of duty which are substantially higher than the average. They are normally applied to sensitive products.

tariff quota. A European Community system allowing limited amounts of certain goods to be imported from outside the European Community at reduced or nil rates of duty and/or Common Agricultural Policy (**q.v.**) charges.

tariffication. A system under which members of GATT (**q.v.**) would try to establish a tariff equivalent of a non-tariff measure before negotiating it away.

taxable person. A person who makes or intends to make taxable supplies (**q.v.**) and is registered or required to be registered for VAT.

taxable supply. In VAT, a supply of goods or services made in the United Kingdom other than an exempt supply.

taxation of costs. The formal assessment of the costs of legal proceedings, according to a prescribed scale.

taxed costs. The amount held by a taxing master (**q.v.**) to be payable by the unsuccessful party to a civil action.

taxing master. An official of the Supreme Court who supervises the assessment of costs payable by the parties to an action. Appointed from solicitors of at least 10 years' standing.

tax invoice. An invoice in respect of a taxable supply (**q.v.**) for VAT which satisfies the requirements of regulations.

tax on the margin. The margin between purchase price and selling price, where tax is applied to the margin in the case of certain dealers operating second hand schemes.

tax paid. Applied to situations where all taxes have been paid abroad, and have not nor will be refunded.

tax period. A period, generally of three months, in respect of which people registered for VAT must make a return.

tax point. The time at which a taxable supply (**q.v.**) is to be treated as taking place for the purposes of the charge to VAT.

tax return. A form which must be furnished by a taxable person at the end of each accounting period, accounting for that person's VAT situation.

tax year. In respect of a taxable person (**q.v.**) for VAT, any period of 12 calendar months commencing on the day following the end of that person's first tax year or any succeeding period of 12 calendar months.

tea. Zero-rated for VAT as food of a kind used for human consumption (Sch. 5, VATA).

temporary importation (TI). The bringing of goods, including vehicles and other means of transport, into the customs territory of a country, when they will be exported subject to certain conditions.

temporary visitor. A person normally resident outside the United Kingdom who, at the time of his entry, intends to remain temporarily without becoming normally resident.

tenancy. A leasehold interest in land, usually for a fixed term of years, and less than absolute ownership.

tenancy at sufferance. A situation arising where a person continues in possession after his contractual tenancy has come to an end.

tenancy at will. The grant of possession by an owner to a tenant for so long as either pleases, and terminable by notice or an act inconsistent with tenancy.

tenancy from year to year. Tenancy created by grant or implication requiring six month's notice.

tenancy in common. Where property is owned in agreed shares by several persons, and on his death the share of each owner passes to his personal representative.

tenant for life. Someone entitled to enjoy the benefit of property during his own or someone else's life.

tender. A response made to an advertisement asking for quotations to supply goods or to carry out works.

ten-minute rule. The procedure under which a brief discussion of the case for and against the introduction of a bill into the House of Commons can be made, in the hope that it will be sponsored later.

tents. Sweet red wines from Spain.

term. An expression describing elements of contracts of varying importance, such as conditions and warranties.

terminal market. Supplies of goods and services in the course of dealings on terminal markets are zero-rated.

term of years absolute. A leasehold interest.

tertiary legislation. Sub-delegated legislation. Customs and Excise purport to issue publications having the force of law, which have not been the subject of any Parliamentary consideration.

testate succession. The transfer of a person's property on death according to the terms of his will.

territorial straits. Straits of land between which no high seas (**q.v.**) exist, but where the intervening sea is entirely within the territorial limits of one or more countries.

territorial waters. The area of adjacent sea over which a country claims to exercise territorial jurisdiction. The limits vary widely throughout the world.

test case. Where a number of actions are mounted against the same defendant in respect of the same circumstances, one case may be selected to test the issues.

testator. A man who has made a will (as opposed to a female, known as a testatrix).

testatrix. A female who has made a will (as opposed to a male who is known as a testator).

testatum. The clause in a conveyance or lease expressing the consideration (**q.v.**) relating to the transaction.

textiles surveillance body. An organisation within GATT (**q.v.**), established to oversee the operation of the multifibre-arrangement (**q.v.**).

theft. The dishonest appropriation of property belonging to another with the intention of permanently depriving that other of it.

third country. A state outside the customs territory of the European Community (**q.v.**). Also referred to as non-Community countries (**q.v.**).

third country trader. A person carrying on a business who is established in a country other than a member state of the European Community.

third party. A person not originally party to a case who has been joined to it because the original defendant claims that he is involved.

third party liability. The liability of an insured person to compensate someone who has sustained loss by his actions or the actions of persons under him.

thoroughfare town. Towns on the London-Dover and London-Berwick posting routes where members of the Vintner's Company of the City of London could sell wine without a justices or excise licence.

three-fourths r-dc (running-down clause). A clause in a policy of marine insurance making underwriters liable for three-fourths of any damage that the owner of the insured vessel may be obliged to pay to the owner of another vessel because of a collision.

threshold price. An expression used for Common Market purposes to denote the lowest price at which certain articles can be imported into the EEC.

through bill of lading. A bill of lading (**q.v.**) which provides for the carriage of goods from one place to another by a series of forms of transport.

tied house. A public house subject to an agreement to buy all its beer from a particular brewery.

tied oil. Hydrocarbon oil (**q.v.**) which has been allowed to be delivered duty free to a bonded user or bonded distributor (**q.v.**).

time charter. An agreement in the form of charter-party (**q.v.**) under which the ship is hired for a certain period of time.

time of supply. The time when a supply of goods or services is treated as taking place for VAT purposes.

time policy. A policy, generally of marine insurance, protecting the subject-matter for a fixed period of time.

TIR (Transport International Routier). A system involving the issue of carnets to road hauliers allowing them to take loaded vehicles across national frontiers with minimum customs formalities.

tithes. Payments in respect of land which until 1925 varied with the rise and fall of the price of corn.

title. The right of ownership.

tobacco port. A port approved by the Commissioners of Customs and Excise for the importation of tobacco.

tobacco products. Any of the following: cigarettes, cigars, hand-rolling tobacco (**q.v.**), other smoking tobacco, chewing tobacco. Herbal smoking products are not included.

tobacco products duty. An excise duty on tobacco products (**q.v.**).

Tokyo Round. The seventh round of multilateral trade negotiations of GATT (**q.v.**) which took place between 1973 and 1979.

tonnage and poundage. Legislation introduced at the Restoration to grant Charles II customs duties for the defence of English merchant vessels at sea.

tonnage dues. Changes made by a port authority on a ship entering its limits, which are calculated according to its registered tonnage.

tontine policy. A policy of life assurance where no bonus is payable if death takes place before the end of a stated period.

tons register. The tons of a ship's net tonnage ascertained and registered according to merchant shipping regulations.

topographical plans. Topographical plans are zero-rated for VAT (Sch. 5, VATA).

tort. Literally 'a wrong'; in law a breach of a duty created by the law which gives rise to an action at the hands of the aggrieved person.

tortfeasor. One who has committed a civil wrong giving rise to an action in law.

tortious act. An act giving rise to a cause of action for a civil wrong.

tour operation. The application of VAT legislation may in certain circumstances be modified in the case of tour operators, including travel agents acting as principals and any other person providing for the benefit of travellers services of a kind commonly provided by tour operators or travel agents.

towage. The charge levied for the use of a tug to help a ship move in or out of harbour.

towage services. Towage services are zero-rated for VAT (Sch. 5, VATA).

tower's liability clause. In policies of marine insurance, a provision covering liability for damage caused while a tug is towing another vessel.

towing and salving clause. A provision in a contract for the charter of a ship to cover the giving and receiving of tows, and other emergency situations.

town customs. Duties levied on goods by a city or town in former times to maintain public works such as bridges, quays and harbours.

trade descriptions legislation. Laws making it an offence to apply to goods a false description in the course of trading.

trade round. A multilateral negotiation held to a prescribed plan and timetable, intended to improve trade rules and exchange concessions in a variety of areas.

trademark. (1) A mark used on or in connection with goods in order to demonstrate that they belong to the owner of the trade mark. (2) The transfer or assignment of a trademark is regarded as a service supplied where received for VAT purposes.

trademark register. An official record of trademarks which is maintained at the Patent Office.

trader. Customs terminology for any taxpayer, taxable person or person liable to any of the Department's taxes or duties. Applied indiscriminately to any individual, firm or company, whatever its size.

trader sealing. The authorisation by Customs and Excise for traders to use their own seals in place of official customs seals for securing goods under customs control.

trade union. The supply to members of a trade union of services and connected goods referable to its aims and available without payment other than through a membership subscription is exempt from VAT (Sch. 6, VATA).

trading certificate. A certification from the Registrar of Companies that a company is entitled to commence business.

trading stamp scheme. VAT rules are modified to provide for the valuation of a trading stamp as consideration for the goods exchanged for them.

tramp ship. A trading vessel at liberty to carry freight all over the world, and not on any particular line.

transfer of a going concern. A system under which the transfer of a business from one concern to another can be relieved of liability for VAT.

transfer of residence (TOR). The permanent transfer into a customs territory of a person's personal and household effects (including vehicles), subject to certain conditions.

transire. A declaration giving details of his cargo which the master of a ship carrying cargo around the coast of Britain must lodge with Customs and Excise prior to departure.

transit goods. Goods on a ship or aircraft not to be delivered on arrival at a particular location, but to be carried further.

transmission clause. A clause in a company's articles giving the personal representatives of a deceased shareholder the right either to transfer shares to themselves without registration, or to have themselves registered.

transmission of shares. The automatic transfer of shares by operation of law in such circumstances as the death, bankruptcy or unsoundness of mind of the shareholder.

transparency. The principle that national policy measures affecting international trade should be apparent to and open to scrutiny by trading partners.

transit shed. A place for the deposit of goods not yet cleared out of customs charge.

transport. Certain types of transport are zero-rated for VAT (Sch. 5, VATA).

trans-shipment. The transfer of goods between one vehicle, ship or aircraft before the final destination has been reached.

travaux preparatoires. Preparatory drafts and discussions relating to legislation which may be considered in interpreting EEC law but not British acts of Parliament.

traveller's cheque. A draft drawn by the holder for an amount in sterling, to be cashed by the foreign associates of the issuing bank at the current rate of exchange.

traveller's letter of credit. A request by an issuing bank to its associates abroad to issue cash to the holder up to a specified amount.

treasure trove. A term applied to concealed gold or silver of which the owner is unknown, and which is accordingly deemed to belong to the Crown.

treasury. The Department of State responsible for administration and control of state expenditure.

treasury bill. A type of Government security which in 1897 replaced the Exchequer Bill.

treasury bench. The front bench of the Government side in the House of Commons.

treaty. A formal agreement between two or more countries.

treaty of accession. The instrument by which the United Kingdom joined the Common Market in 1972.

Treaty of Rome. The original agreement by which the Common Market was first established in 1957.

treaty port. An expression formerly applied to places in China which were open to foreign trade.

treaty re-insurance. An arrangement between insurers and reinsurers by which the latter can accept or decline a proportion of any risk over the insurer's limit.

trente et quarante. A game in respect of which gaming licence duty is payable for any premises on which it is played.

trespass to goods. The unlawful interference by one person with the property of another person.

triangulation. A system under which goods can be despatched from the European Community (**q.v.**) by being exported from one member state, and returned to the Community by being imported into another member state.

tribunal centre. An administrative office of VAT tribunals.

tribunal chairman. The person who heads the judicial function of a VAT tribunal (**q.v.**) sitting to hear a VAT appeal (**q.v.**).

Trinity House. The chief lighthouse authority in the United Kingdom also the pilotage authority for the Thames, English Channel and certain other areas.

Trinity Master. A senior member of Trinity House (**q.v.**) who acts as nautical adviser in maritime cases.

trust. An interest in property whereby one person is bound in conscience to hold or administer property for the benefit of another person.

trust corporation. Corporations such as clearing banks, and some large insurance companies authorised to act as trustees.

trustee. A person bound in conscience to hold or administer property for the benefit of another person.

trustee and personal representative costs. The basis of assessment of costs in legal proceedings where one of the parties is either a trustee (**q.v.**) or a personal representative (**q.v.**).

trust for sale. Created where it is ultimately intended that land shall be sold, but where the trustees enjoy the same powers as a tenant for life.

trust of imperfect obligation. A trust which cannot be enforced by a particular beneficiary, for example a pet cat in whose favour the trust has been established.

trust territory. A territory administered under the supervision of a country appointed by the United Nations.

trustee in bankruptcy. A trustee in bankruptcy can in certain circumstances be separately registered for VAT.

turbary. An ancient right to dig turves on certain land.

TURN. A Trader's Unique Reference Number allocated by Customs and Excise.

turnkey agreement. In industrial contracts, an agreement for the supply of the complete range of material or equipment necessary.

turnover. The total sales of a business for a particular period.

twopenny ale. A malt ale or beer much appreciated in Scotland in earlier times, so much that in the Act of Union it was exempted from increases in duty.

Tynwald. The Parliament of the Isle of Man, which is responsible for VAT legislation in that island.

U

UKREP. The United Kingdom Permanent Representative to the European Community (**q.v.**).

ullage. The amount of liquid lacking in a barrel which is only partly full.

ultra vires. Any exercise of powers in excess of those laid down in governing documentation or legislation.

***ultra vires* borrowing.** Borrowing by the directors of a company in excess of the limit authorised by its memorandum of association.

unaltered goods. Imported goods put in for inward processing relief or processing for free circulation but which have not been processed.

unauthorised issue of invoice. A civil penalty in VAT law. A person is liable to be assessed for the amount shown on an unauthorised invoice.

uncalled capital. That part of the value of shares in a limited company which has not been called for to pay up.

U.N.C.T.A.D. The United Nations Commission on Trade and Development which concerns itself with trading problems of developing states, particularly in the third world.

under insurance. Insurance for an amount less than the agreed valuation or the insurable value of property.

underlease. A later or sub-lease created by the occupier or tenant holding under the original lease.

underproof. The strength of spirits in which the proportion of alcohol is less than in proof spirit.

underwriter. A person undertaking to make the payment (the insurer) in a contract of marine insurance. Generally, a person undertaking to make up a deficiency, for example, the remainder of an issue of shares not taken up.

undischarged bankrupt. A debtor who has been discharged bankrupt, and who commits a criminal offence if he obtains credit for more than a certain amount without disclosing that fact.

undisclosed principal. A person on behalf of whom an agent acts, but whose existence is not known to the third person at the time of making the contract.

undue influence. Use by person of a power over another person to induce the second person to take a certain course of action.

unenforceable. The condition of not being enforceable by legal action.

U.N.E.S.C.O.. The United Nations Educational, Scientific and Cultural Organisation, a UN specialised agency with its headquarters in Paris responsible for international development in these areas.

unidentifiable cargo. Goods which arrive at their destination so badly damaged that they cannot be identified.

unincorporated association. A group of individuals existing to further common interests e.g. a photographic club, a Chamber of Commerce.

unit of account. A device to establish single common prices for accounting purposes within the Common Market.

United Kingdom waters. Any waters, including inland waters, within the seaward limits of the territorial sea of the United Kingdom.

United Nations charter. The formal agreement to which nations subscribing to the United Nations Organisation adhere.

United Nations goods. No tax is payable on the importation of certain goods produced by the United Nations or one of its organisations.

United Nations Organisation (U.N.O.). The current world association of independent states, founded after the Second World War, with its main headquarters in New York.

universal agent. An agent whose authority is completely unrestricted.

university. The provision of education or research by a university is exempt from VAT (Sch. 6, VATA).

unjust enrichment. A defence which Customs and Excise may raise in a case where they would otherwise have to repay overpaid VAT (**q.v.**).

unlimited company. A company the members of which have no limit on their liability to contribute in the event of winding-up.

unlimited legal tender. Money which can be offered or tendered up to a particular stated amount.

unliquidated claim. An allegation that an unfixed or uncertain sum of money is due.

unliquidated damages. Damages which the court itself fixes.

unneutral service. The act of a neutral merchant ship in time of war by aiding an enemy in some way, or breaking a blockade.

unsecured debenture. Debenture capital (**q.v.**) which is not charged on the assets of a company, but taken only on the basis of a promise to repay the loan taken.

unseaworthiness. For purposes of marine insurance, the condition of a ship which is unfitted to withstand the normal perils of the sea.

unrebated oil. Oil on which the full amount of excise duty has been paid and on which no rebate has been allowed.

unvalued policy. An insurance policy which does not set a value on the items insured, but leaves it to be fixed within the limit of the agreement.

usage. A particular course of dealing usual in a certain occupation or area of business life.

utmost good faith (*uberrimae fidei*). The principle that a complete disclosure must be made of all relevant matters, particularly in relation to insurance.

usquebaugh (uisge beatha). The Gaelic for whisky, literally "The water of life". It was applied in Ireland and the Highlands, as opposed to spirits distilled in the Lowlands which were known as 'aqua vitae' (also 'water of life').

usual place of residence. In relation to a body corporate, for purposes of VAT registration means the place where it is legally constituted.

usual residence. For certain reliefs, the place or country in which a person spends a prescribed minimum period of time each year because of work or personal connection.

usury. The lending of money at an exorbitant rate of interest.

utter. To distribute something false or illegal, for example to utter counterfeit coinage.

V

vacant possession. In respect of land or housing, the state of being free from occupation so that a new owner or tenant can move in.

valuation declaration. A form on which an importer declares the method of valuation and the elements involved in calculating the value for import duty purposes.

value added tax. An indirect tax charged on the supply of goods or services made in the United Kingdom.

value of supply. The value for VAT purposes of a supply of goods or services.

valued policy. A policy, generally in respect of marine insurance, setting out the agreed value of the subject-matter insured.

variable charge (VC). A special charge comprising a fixed element and a variable element. It applies to goods processed from certain basic agricultural products.

variable import levy. A device of the Common Market for the purposes of its Common Agricultural Policy (**q.v.**) to bring prices of imports up to the level sought to be maintained inside the EEC.

variation of trust. A scheme for the re-arrangement of the terms of a trust in the interests of the beneficiaries.

VATA. A contraction used to describe the Value Added Tax Act of 1983.

VAT account. An account which a taxable person (**q.v.**) is obliged to pay as part of his required accounts and records.

VAT appeal. An appeal to a VAT tribunal (**q.v.**) on one of the grounds set out in s. 40, VATA.

VAT fraction. A formula applied to determine the amount of standard-rated VAT payable on a VAT inclusive sum.

VAT fraud. The fraudulent evasion of VAT, which may be subject to either criminal or civil penalties.

VAT group. A group of associated companies registered under a representative member (**q.v.**) in order to obtain preferential VAT treatment.

VAT rate. The rate at which VAT is for the time being charged. Between Finance Acts it may be varied by up to 25% by Treasury Order.

VAT return. The form on which a registered taxable person must account for VAT at the end of each VAT period.

VAT tribunal. A special court established to adjudicate on appeals by the public against decisions of Customs and Excise on VAT liability and assessment.

VAT tribunals reports (VAT TR). The official law reports of cases heard in the VAT tribunals, and sanctioned by the President of VAT tribunals.

VAT warehouse. A distiller's warehouse (**q.v.**) approved for the storage of spirits in vats.

vatable. A supply which is chargeable to VAT at the standard rate, (or, in strict terms, zero-rate).

vatting. The admixing of spirits in a vat to secure uniformity of character.

vehicles excise duty. The licence fee charged annually to permit a vehicle to be on public roads (**q.v.**).

veil of incorporation. The principle that a company is a distinct legal entity from its members.

verification of flag. In international law, the right of a warship to pursue and investigate another ship which is suspected of sailing under false colours.

verjuice. Juice taken from sour grapes or apples which is unfit for making into wine or cider.

vertical integration. The combining of a number of businesses each following a different stage in the production process within the same industry.

vesting assent. A document vesting settled land in a tenant for life.

vesting order. In bankruptcy, an order made vesting disclaimed property (**q.v.**) in a person having an interest in it.

vexatious litigant. A person who persistently and without reasonable cause starts legal proceedings may be so declared, and may then only start cases with permission of a court.

vicarious liability. The liability of one person for wrongful acts committed by another.

vicarious performance. Where the person making a promise can rely on it being carried out by someone else.

vice-president of VAT tribunals. The person appointed to deputise for the president of VAT tribunals (**q.v.**).

victualling bill. The document which a ship's captain must give to Customs and Excise before sailing for a foreign destination. It lists all dutiable goods to be used on the voyage.

victualling warehouse. A warehouse for the receipt of Common Agricultural Policy (**q.v.**) goods, to be supplied as stores to vessels or aircraft or deep-sea drilling and extraction platforms and associated workpoints.

vingt-et-un. A game in respect of which gaming licence duty is payable for premises on which it is played.

visible trade. The export and import of goods.

visiting forces. A body, contingent or detachment of overseas forces for the time being present in the United Kingdom on the invitation of the government. They may in certain circumstances be entitled to personal relief (**q.v.**) from duty and/or VAT on importation.

void. The state of being without legal effect.

voidable. Capable of being made without legal effect at the option of a particular person.

voir dire. A preliminary examination of a witness or a juror, usually carried out by a judge, to see if the person is capable of fulfilling his function.

voluntary bill of indictment. A means of bringing a serious criminal charge to trial in a Crown Court without going through a committal (Q.V.).

voluntary excess. The amount of any loss which a person taking out an insurance policy agrees that he will find for himself.

voluntary restraint agreement. An export restraint introduced voluntarily to avoid disruption to a particular market.

voluntary winding-up. The dissolution of a company brought about at the request of the company itself.

voyage. For the purposes of maritime law, the trip out and the trip home taken together.

voyage charter. A contract for the hire of a ship for a single voyage.

voyage in home waters. In relation to a ship, a voyage in which the ship is at all times either at sea or within the limits of a port.

voyage policy. A policy of marine insurance under which the subject-matter is protected for the duration of a specified voyage.

W

wager policy. A form of insurance policy unenforceable in England, but not in some foreign states. The interest of the person insuring in the goods insured is very slender, or non-existent.

wagering contract. A promise to give something to another person on the ascertainment of an uncertain event in which neither has an interest.

waiver. Where persons who were in the course of entering an agreement both decide to abandon their rights under it.

walking possession agreement. An agreement between Customs and Excise and a VAT debtor that the debtor acknowledges the distress, and undertakes not to allow the goods to be removed.

want of prosecution. The process by which a civil claim or criminal prosecution may be discussed because the person making it has not taken the matter further.

war contraband. In international law, goods which may not be shipped to belligerents (**q.v.**) without liability to seizure if captured.

war grave. Articles connected with war graves may be subject to relief from VAT on importation.

war risks. In policies of insurance the dangers stemming from actual military operations.

warehoused. Warehoused or rewarehoused in an excise warehouse.

warehousekeeper. The occupier of an approved customs warehouse who has entered a bond for the payment of duties chargeable on goods deposited in his warehouse, and who is responsible for observing the law and any conditions imposed.

warehousing. The placing of goods in an approved warehouse (**q.v.**), on which duty and import VAT does not have to be paid so long as they remain there.

warehouse to warehouse. A policy of marine insurance by which goods are covered from the warehouse of consignment, through the entire transit to final delivery at the warehouse of destination.

warranty. An element in a contract of less importance than a condition (**q.v.**). Failure to carry out a warranty will not defeat the contract.

warranty of neutrality. In policies of marine insurance, an implication that the vessel and its cargo will be of neutral character throughout a voyage.

wash. Distiller's wort (**q.v.**) in which fermentation has begun.

wash back. A vessel in which wort (**q.v.**) is collected, and fermented into wash (**q.v.**).

wash charger. A vessel in which wash (**q.v.**) is collected from the wash backs (**q.v.**) for removal to the still (**q.v.**).

waste. Unlawful damage comitted or allowed by an occupier of land to the detriment of others having an interest in the land.

wasting asset. Property, the actual value of which diminishes as time passes, for example a leasehold.

water. Certain types of water are zero-rated for VAT (Sch. 5, VATA).

water authority. A body which may be entitled to refund of VAT in certain circumstances under s. 20, VATA.

water development board. A body which may be entitled to a refund of VAT in certain circumstances under s. 20, VATA.

water/gas. Zero-rated for VAT as fuel and power (Sch. 5, VATA).

weather permitting clause. In contractual agreement, a provision preventing time being counted where adverse weather conditions have prevented performance.

weather working day. In contracts where performance depends on fair weather, a day on which work was not interrupted by adverse weather conditions.

weekly bills of mortality. Weekly returns of births and deaths published in the parishes of London every Thursday prior to the establishment of the Register of Births, Deaths and Marriages in 1846.

weights and measures legislation. Laws containing a general provision against the giving of short weight, even though no fraud can be proved.

welfare services. The supply otherwise than for profit by a charity or public body of welfare services and goods connected therewith is exempt from VAT (Sch. 6, VATA).

Welsh National Water Development Authority. A body to which in certain circumstances a refund of VAT may be made.

wharfage. A charge made for depositing goods on a wharf.

wheel of fortune. A game in respect of which gaming licence duty is payable for premises on which it is played.

whisky (whiskey). Spirits distilled from a mash of cereals which has been saccharified by the diastase of malt in it, fermented by the action of yeast, distilled at an alcoholic strength below 94.8% and matured in wooden casks in a warehouse for at least three years.

whisky refund scheme. A European Community system of refunds on Community cereals used in whisky for export outside the European Community.

white slaving. The procuring of women for the purposes of prostitution.

whole account policy. A form of bad-debt insurance, covering losses up to an agreed percentage of total sales.

whole life policy. A contract of assurance (**q.v.**) where it is agreed that the sum assured is payable only on the death of the life assured.

wholesaler. One who purchases goods in large quantities from manufacturers and sells on to retailers in smaller amounts.

wholly owned subsidiary. A company which has no members other than another company which owns it.

widower's duty. An assessed tax levied according to social position on all childless widowers not receiving charitable support. It lasted from 1695 until 1706.

winding-up. The normal method of dissolution of a company, either because of insolvency, or because the purpose for which it existed came to an end.

winding-up order. A formal order made by the Court for the dissolution of a company.

winding-up petition. The formal means by which a compulsory dissolution of a company by the Court is put into motion.

window duty. The number of windows was the criteria for assessing the Inhabited House Duty from 1696 until that duty was abolished in 1834. Thereafter a Window Duty continued until 1851.

wine. Any liquor obtained from the alcoholic fermentation of fresh grapes or their must (whether or not the liquor is fortified with spirits).

wine lees. Dregs of wine.

winery. The premises, places, rooms and vessels in respect of which an excise entry is made in the course of production of wine and made-wine.

winery warehouse. A warehouse at a winery approved by Customs and Excise for the duty-free storage of alcoholic liquors used in the production of wine or made-wine (**q.v.**).

wire and plomb seal. An official customs seal consisting of a circular lead seal into which is looped a length of lashed steel wire, and closed by a plombing press.

wireless sets for the blind. Wireless sets for the blind are zero-rated for VAT (Sch. 5, VATA).

working capital. The excess of current assets over current liabilities.

World Health Organisation (WHO). A specialised agency of the United Nations (**q.v.**) responsible for research and development in medical matters.

work of art. The disposal of certain limited categories of works of art is exempt from VAT (Sch. 6, VATA). In other cases, supplies of works of art are subject to a margin scheme (**q.v.**) and only subject to VAT on the margin between acquisition and disposal prices.

worm. A copper pipe connecting the head of a still with the safe in a distillery.

wort. The liquid obtained by dissolving sugar or molasses in water or by extracting the soluble portion of malt or corn during brewing.

wreck. Generally applied to anything without an obvious owner, on or in the sea, or cast up by it.

wreck commissioner. A member of a special court set up to investigate shipwreck.

wreck report. The details which must be given by the captain of any ship arriving in the UK of any wreck or derelict vessel met during the voyage.

wreckage. Any material which has been thrown up on a shore after a shipwreck.

writ of assistance. An authority issued to officers of Customs and Excise in certain circumstances to enter premises, by force if necessary, and take up goods or documents.

writ of summons. A document the issue of which commences a civil case in the High Court.

Y

Yaounde convention. An international agreement between the founder states of the Common Market and certain of their former territories, by which the latter would be allowed tariff reductions on importation of their products.

year's purchase. The rent, profit or income during a year used as a merit of valuation.

yield. The return on an investment from dividend or interest expressed as a percentage of its market price or cost.

youth custody order. A sentence of detention now imposed on a young offender for a specified period, in place of the previous Borstal order.

Yorkshire Water Authority. A body which in certain circumstances may be entitled to a refund of VAT.

youth club. The provision by a youth club of the facilities available to its members is exempt from VAT (Sch. 6, VATA).

Z

zero-rate. A nil rate of VAT applied in UK law to certain supplies of goods and services.

zone time. A standard of time to be applied at sea, dependent on the time zone in which a vessel is positioned.